Postcard History Series

Petaluma
in Vintage Postcards

THE CARNEGIE PUBLIC LIBRARY. One of Petaluma's finest public buildings, this former town library was completed in 1906 with a competitive Carnegie Foundation grant, similar to other "Free Public Library" projects across the country. Addie Atwater, president of the Ladies Improvement Club, was the civic leader who spearheaded this effort and sold the land to the city for half its market value. The two-story Neoclassical-style building was designed by local architect Brainerd Jones. (Authors' collection.)

ON THE FRONT COVER: DOWNTOWN PETALUMA. The early buildings on Main Street were wooden structures and included grocery and provision stores as well as hardware merchants and livery stables. By the late 1800s, Petaluma had grown into an industrial and commercial town with the presence of banks, hotels, and theater buildings. This postcard is of Main Street looking north in 1922 with the Masonic Lodge building and the original clock tower on the left. Main Street was renamed Petaluma Boulevard in 1958. (Authors' collection.)

ON THE BACK COVER: "PETALUMA'S SIGHT-SEEING BUS." This image of a truck transporting chickens was made into a postcard to promote Petaluma's fame as the "World's Egg Basket." Handwritten on the back of the card is this statement: "I doubt if we ever go to town unless late in the day that we don't see loads of chickens." (Authors' collection.)

POSTCARD HISTORY SERIES

Petaluma in Vintage Postcards

Alice van Ommeren and KC Greaney

ARCADIA
PUBLISHING

ISBN 978-1-4671-0544-6

Published by Arcadia Publishing
Charleston, South Carolina

Printed in the United States of America

Library of Congress Control Number: 2020934186

For all general information contact Arcadia Publishing at:
Telephone 843-853-2070
Fax 843-853-0044
E-mail sales@arcadiapublishing.com
For customer service and orders:
Toll-Free 1-888-313-2665

Visit us on the Internet at www.arcadiapublishing.com

Chicken Ranch at Petaluma. This vintage card, postmarked from the USS *Pensacola* and dated 1909, shows a bucolic scene of a chicken ranch with two women feeding a large flock of mostly white leghorn hens. Behind them is a row of "colony houses," a Petaluma poultry farming innovation. The message on the back of the postcard reads, "Dear Pa: Does the scene on the other side look good to you? I suppose you still think there is money in chickens." (Authors' collection.)

CONTENTS

Acknowledgments

The Petaluma Historical Library and Museum was an invaluable resource to the authors, with special thanks to Solange Russek, museum collection manager, who provided postcards from the museum's collection for inclusion in this book. Thanks also to Katherine Rinehart, who contributed images of postcards from the Sonoma County History and Genealogy Library, and Connie Williams at the Petaluma Library. Longtime postcard collectors Craig Blackstone, Lew Baer, and Gail Unzelman also contributed images to this book, for which we are grateful. Unless otherwise noted in the captions, all other postcards are from the authors' collection.

We discovered relevant information from many sources, primarily the research archives at the Petaluma Historical Library and Museum, the Petaluma History Room at the Petaluma branch of the Sonoma County Library, and the resources listed in the bibliography of this book. We had conversations and insight from many others, including Solange Russek, Terry Park, Abraham Solar, and Frank Maack.

Terry Park was a valuable source of detailed information with a keen eye for editing. We would also like to thank Linda Buffo, Leif and Sherri Ortgren, Susan Coolidge, Solange Russek, Barbara Maxwell, and Sandy Wilkins for reviewing parts or all of the text and related postcard images.

To support further efforts to preserve Petaluma's history, the royalties from this book go to the Petaluma Historical Library and Museum.

INTRODUCTION

In its first decades after incorporation in 1858, Petaluma was the largest and most affluent settlement in the North Bay. This was due in great part to the town's fortunate location at the terminus of a waterway that led to the San Pablo and San Francisco Bays, rendering it an important transportation and thus commercial hub during the population explosion in California created by the Gold Rush. The development of commercially viable incubators in 1879 resulted in substantial growth of the local poultry industry by the early 1900s. The chamber of commerce's innovative marketing in the 1920s put Petaluma on the map as the "World's Egg Basket." Because of the success of the chicken ranches as well as other agricultural and industrial endeavors and its location as a transportation hub, Petaluma continued as an important commercial center.

These successful industries provided the capital for residents, organizations, and businesses to invest in stately homes, beautiful churches, community parks, and other civic institutions. When the poultry industry moved to large-scale factory farms in Central and Southern California and other states by the mid-20th century and trucks over roads became the preferred mode of transportation, Petaluma lost some advantages. Yet the city evolved, and many beautiful historic buildings remain due to preservation efforts. Remarkably, Petaluma's historic downtown district is listed in the National Register of History Places, along with several other individual residential, civic, and commercial buildings.

The purpose of this book is to showcase vintage postcards of Petaluma, which we have placed in a historical context. This collection illustrates Petaluma's identity, as postcards were mass-produced visual advertisements. The popularity of postcards coincides with Petaluma's growth and development in the early 1900s. The vintage postcards in this book illustrate Petaluma's transformation from a pioneer town to an industrious city, as well as the unique strategies used to promote Petaluma via the poultry industry.

Privately printed postcards were first introduced in 1898, when Congress passed the Private Mailing Card Act. The act lowered the postal rates on private cards, which increased their demand. Until 1907, the backs of postcards only allowed for the recipient's address, leaving the front for the image and the message. In 1907, postcards with a divided back were permitted, which meant the address and message shared space on the back, and the image on the postcard could now take up the entire front. This modification increased the popularity of postcards, launching an era referred to by postcard collectors as the "Golden Age of Postcards."

During this period, the majority of postcards were printed in Germany, where lithography was considered an art and the printing presses were more advanced than the ones in the United

States. The beginning of World War I caused imports from Germany to decline, and the nation's interest in postcards began to diminish. Cards continued to be published in the United States, but their quality dropped, and demand for them decreased.

Around 1930, "linen" postcards began to be printed on textured paper with a linen-like surface. In 1939, the photochrome, or "chrome," postcard was introduced and is still used today. These cards have glossy finishes and are easily produced using color photography. Real-photo postcards, also known as mailable photographs, were used as early as 1900. These cards, produced in small amounts by publishers or individuals, were expensive to produce and were generally less common. Several businesses used the popularity of postcards in the early 1900s to advertise their products and services.

The collection of postcards in this book illustrates Petaluma's history from the mid-19th century through the first decades of the 20th century, when postcards were popular. This book does not provide the complete history of Petaluma, as many important historical events are not represented in postcards. There are few postcards from before 1900, so the important history of the original inhabitants, the Coast Miwok people, is unfortunately not included. Nor are the Spanish or Mexican eras of California well represented in postcards. The book nevertheless provides a comprehensive illustration of how vintage postcards document important aspects of Petaluma history.

Due to Petaluma's decision to promote itself as the "World's Egg Basket," there are many postcards showcasing chickens and eggs. We would like to conclude this introduction with a poem extolling the importance of the poultry industry and all it brought to town. Written by W.O. Manwaring, this poem, "Petaluma Hen," was published in the *Argus-Courier* 85th Anniversary & Progress Edition, May 4, 1941:

I am a Leghorn hen!
Proudly I stand!

For in the march of men
To pioneer this land;

Millions upon millions of my clan
Served unceasingly

Laid increasingly
To build for man.

Our feathered numbers ever growing,
Like white, living waters flowing

Through Sonoma's rolling hills.
And with us grew her stores and mills;

Grew a little country town;
Grew a place of world renown;

Grew PETALUMA, City of Men—
Built by Her Majesty, THE HEN!

One

The Fairest Land in All the World

Early History

The Petaluma Creek. Originally called the Petaluma Creek, the waterway is technically an estuary of the San Pablo Bay with a daily tidal fluctuation of about seven feet. In 1833, a young Mexican ensign Mariano Guadalupe Vallejo scouted the North Bay for settlement, and described Petaluma thusly: "I have made it to paradise—the fairest land in all the world. Nothing in all California was comparable; everything was ready-made for civilization—soil, climate, abundant water, a great harbor, opportunity for commerce with the world, and for landscape, for variety, a land of pure enchantment."

BAY AREA TRANSPORTATION LINES. This map from 1910 shows the major rail lines and waterways around the San Francisco Bay, including the Petaluma Creek in the upper left of the postcard. Petaluma's strategic location along a navigable waterway and proximity to San Francisco made it an important port town. By about 1900, the Petaluma Creek was the third-largest shipping waterway in California, after the Sacramento and San Joaquin Rivers.

FORT ROSS. In 1808, the Russian ship *Kadiak* explored the Sonoma coast to identify a location for a possible trading post, primarily to support the hunting of sea otter for their prized pelts. In 1812, a site 13 miles north of the Russian River was chosen, what was to become Fort Ross. Built of redwood, there were nine buildings within the walls and fifty without. Two bastions and forty-one cannons were also installed, making the trading post appear to be a military stronghold.

THE SONOMA MISSION. Founded in 1823, Mission San Francisco Solano de Sonoma is the last of the 21 Franciscan missions in Alta California and the only one established under Mexican rule. Gen. Mariano Guadalupe Vallejo was charged with secularizing the mission in 1834 and settling the North Bay, in part to fend off the perceived threat of Russian encroachment from Fort Ross. Thus, Fort Ross and the mission in Sonoma were the impetuses for non-native settlement of the town of Sonoma as well as Petaluma. (Courtesy Craig Blackstone.)

VALLEJO'S ADOBE. In an attempt to settle Northern California, in 1834 Gen. Mariano Guadalupe Vallejo was granted 10 square leagues of land or 44,280 acres in his chosen location, Petaluma. The land grant encompassed the area between Petaluma and Sonoma, from just south of Santa Rosa to San Pablo Bay. Large land grants were typical in the Spanish and Mexican periods of California history, in part as payment to government officials as money was scarce. At the time the building was completed in 1836, the Vallejo adobe (named the Rancho Petaluma) was the largest adobe structure in Alta California. While the Vallejos lived most of their time at their home in Sonoma, they spent many weeks at the adobe, sometimes to escape the summer heat, where they hosted many guests and held fandangos or large parties. The Rancho Petaluma was both a social and economic hub in Alta California.

RANCHO PETALUMA. Built primarily by local Indians from the secularized Mission San Francisco Solano in Sonoma, the adobe consisted of a large two-story building forming a U-shape with an open courtyard in the middle. A second structure meant to enclose the courtyard was never completed. Building materials were locally sourced, including native fieldstone for the foundation, redwood from nearby forests for beams and shingles, and adobe brick made on-site. The walls are 3 feet thick and 20 feet high and support a broad two-story veranda around the interior and exterior of the buildings. The Petaluma adobe was a working ranch, raising cattle for the lucrative hide and tallow trade and growing crops such as wheat. At its peak, the Rancho Petaluma employed 600–2,000 workers, primarily Indians from the secularized mission, and had 10,000 head of cattle and 4,000 horses. Trade occurred primarily with merchant ships from the east coast of the United States and Europe. (Above, courtesy Craig Blackstone.)

Decline of the Rancho. Over decades, Vallejo granted portions of his rancho land to others, including some of the earliest white settlers of Petaluma, often as payment for labor and services. After the United States annexed California from Mexico in 1848, contrary to promises outlined in the Treaty of Guadalupe Hidalgo, Spanish and Mexican land grants were no longer legally honored, and squatters from the California Gold Rush flooded California.

New Ownership of the Adobe. Remarkably, in 1857, Vallejo's land title was confirmed by US courts; however, needing money, he sold his adobe and 1,600 acres to William Whiteside of Petaluma. It was purchased again in 1859 by William A. Bliss, a Petaluma attorney, in whose family it remained until acquired by the Native Sons of the Golden West in 1910, when extensive renovation began. The adobe is a National Historic Landmark and was acquired by California State Parks in 1950.

THE PORT OF PETALUMA. The Petaluma Creek featured prominently in the town's history, as it provided transportation and, thus, a means for trade with San Francisco and other ports. Starting off as a rustic frontier trading post, the port town grew with the Gold Rush, and the demand for meat and agricultural products increased, particularly in the city of San Francisco. Petaluma was strategically placed not just as a port, but also in a valley filled with rich farmland and abundant wild game and fowl. In the early years, game, firewood, and, over time, crops like wheat and potatoes were shipped down the river.

Improvements to the River. As the Petaluma Creek was a vital shipping channel for the entire North Bay, its navigability was of great importance. Originally 16 miles from the San Pablo Bay to the town of Petaluma, the creek had many twists and turns, making it difficult to navigate. Early improvements—digging channels to straighten the river—were completed manually, reportedly by Chinese laborers. The creek was declared a river by an act of the US Congress in order to qualify for federally funded dredging. Later improvements were made by the US Army Corps of Engineers, who deepened, widened, and dredged the river in 1880 and 1931. These postcards show "electric suction" dredging efforts by the *Wilmington* in 1914. The postcard above is taken from the foot of Western Avenue, and the one below is "looking north from the new bridge," which would be the double-leaf bascule bridge at Washington Street. (Both, courtesy Petaluma Museum.)

Bridges over the River. Until 1857, the only bridge over the Petaluma Creek was a rickety wooden footbridge north of town at Bridge Street, which was later renamed Lakeville Street. The photograph above (dated 1908) is likely a replacement of the original bridge. By May 1857, a new swing bridge (below) operated across the river at Washington Street. The bridge was built with private funds by the gold-miner-turned-businessman Thomas Hopper, who purchased 270 acres of land in old east Petaluma from General Vallejo on speculation. With the bridge providing reliable transportation across the river, Hopper sold subdivisions for a large profit. In 1883, a second swing bridge was built at D Street, which was not replaced until 1933 with the current steel single-leaf bascule bridge. The Washington Street swing bridge was replaced with a double-leaf bascule bridge in 1913. This second bridge was replaced with the current fixed bridge by 1969.

Further Improvements to the River. This postcard from 1914 shows the cutting of a new channel on the Petaluma Creek, which illustrates ongoing efforts to improve the navigability of the river for commercial purposes. Over the years, many more improvements were made. In 1921, a hairpin curve near downtown was dug out to create a turning basin. As ongoing shoaling creates sandbars and fills in the river, periodic dredging is required for boats of any size to navigate the waterway. (Courtesy Petaluma Museum.)

Two

WHERE RAIL AND WATER TRANSPORTATION MEET

SHIPPING

IMPORTANCE OF THE RIVER. In the decades after the Gold Rush, Petaluma was the largest and most prosperous town in Sonoma County, due in great part to river access to the San Francisco Bay and all the advantages for commerce that came with the strategic location. This postcard shows the paddle wheel steamer *Sonoma* taking on freight. A c. 1914 chamber of commerce brochure pitched Petaluma, "where rail and water transportation meet," as an ideal location for commerce and industry.

The Petaluma and Nearby Ports. The first major port located along the Petaluma Creek was developed by General Vallejo where the Adobe Creek meets the Petaluma Creek, to ferry hides and tallow downstream to ships for export overseas. With the advent of the Gold Rush and the explosion of the population in California, Petaluma primarily provisioned San Francisco and other more local markets via waterways. (Courtesy Craig Blackstone.)

Scow Schooners Hauling Freight. Scores of schooners carried cargo up and down the Petaluma River. This shipping scene shows a schooner having just unloaded lumber. Petalumans also imported grain and feed, hardware, household goods, glass, paper, beer, and later, oyster shells to supplement the poultry diet to harden egg shells. After the cargo of the schooners was unloaded, regional producers shipped exports downriver, including farm and factory goods such as chickens and eggs, incubators, dried fruit, wool, fish, hay, butter, cream, and eggs.

HAY SCOWS. The Petaluma Creek was shallow, especially so during low tide. Scow schooners were popular for hauling freight up and down the river due to their broad unobstructed decks, which facilitated loading and unloading, and their flat bottoms, which minimized getting stuck in muddy sandbars. The flat bottom also allowed the schooner to sit level on the muddy riverbed during low tide. This image shows a schooner headed downstream loaded with hay and a dock piled high with bags of grain. Scow schooners were regionally referred to as "hay scows" because of the prevalence of scows in the San Pablo and San Francisco Bays piled high with hay, locally traveling between Haystack Landing, situated two and a half miles south of downtown Petaluma, to San Francisco's Hay Wharf. (Courtesy Craig Blackstone.)

River Transportation. In 1908, there was a diversity of cargo carriers going up and down the Petaluma River. In addition to 31 schooners, there were at least 3 steamboats (the *Gold*, the *Sonoma*, and the *J.M. White*) and various other fishing boats and barges. This postcard image shows a scow schooner and a fishing smack.

Transportation Connections. Petaluma was the depot and port outlet for the farming industry and grazing interests of the surrounding country. Having connections to transport cargo to and from the river was critical. Warehouses and roads facilitated this process, as did bridges. This image shows the "new" Washington Street Bridge, a double-leaf bascule built in 1913. Note the horse-drawn wagon crossing the bridge. (Courtesy Lew Baer.)

TUGBOATS. This image shows a tugboat, likely the *Golden Eagle*, passing through the Washington Street Bridge with both leaves raised. Tugs were used to pull or push barges, including through narrow bridge openings. (Courtesy Petaluma Museum.)

STEAMERS. Steamships began making the trek to Petaluma in 1852. The steamer *Gold*, pictured here (postmark 1907), was completed in 1883 to run between San Francisco and Petaluma. In that same year, the steamer *Pilot* blew up a few miles below Petaluma, a harsh reminder of the potential dangers of such travel, as seven lives were lost, including Jennie, the first wife of George P. McNear. Still, steamers could haul passengers and more freight and were not dependent on the wind, so they offered advantages over the scow schooners.

Navigating the Petaluma River. This image shows a schooner at a dock and, in the foreground, the muddy banks of the Petaluma River, likely at low tide. Schooners had to time their runs to coincide with the winds and higher tides, and even then, they often bottomed out, requiring workers to use 20-foot poles to push the scow forward. When the river was narrow, two crew members could hop ashore on either side and tow the schooner with slings around their chests connected to the boat by a rope around the front mast. For reasons such as these, in 1878, Petaluma petitioned the US Congress for $25,000 to aid in improving Petaluma Creek. In 1880, the US Army Corps of Engineers widened the creek to 50 feet and deepened it to 3 feet at low tide. Again in 1931, the corps made improvements, further widening and deepening the waterway.

The Turning Basin. In 1921, a hairpin turn was scooped out to create a turning basin, thus allowing larger vessels to come to port and maneuver. This image shows the turning basin, with the Golden Eagle Mill and a grain warehouse in the background.

Transition to Recreational Use. As railroads, bridges, and, eventually, trucks and automobiles connected the North Bay more efficiently to San Francisco and other destinations, there was a decreasing need to ship goods down the river. By the time the Golden Gate Bridge was completed in 1937, trucking had become the more affordable and preferred method of transporting merchandise, significantly diminishing the importance of the Petaluma River for commercial purposes. This postcard illustrates the transition to recreational boats on the Petaluma River.

WHERE WATER AND RAILS MEET. This image shows a spur of the Petaluma & Santa Rosa Railroad built in 1922 on the west side of the Petaluma River at the turning basin, stretching to McNear's warehouse and beyond, with empty boats afloat likely waiting to be loaded. The back of this 1926 postmarked postcard reads, "This is the chicken center of the world. Also a seafront, as a slough reaches up north to here from S.F. Bay." With this river and rail connection, cargo could be unloaded directly from shipping vessels to railroad cars for distribution inland.

"OVER-NIGHT FREIGHT SERVICE." The Petaluma & Santa Rosa Railroad Company provided tug, passenger, and freight service to San Francisco. The company owned the steamers *Gold* and *Petaluma* and made two runs a day to San Francisco. For some time after the railroads were completed, it was still cheaper to ship between Sonoma County and San Francisco via the port of Petaluma.

PETALUMA AND SANTA ROSA RAILROAD COMPANY
OVER-NIGHT FREIGHT SERVICE
— BETWEEN —
SAN FRANCISCO and PETALUMA
LAST —TO— LEAVE
FIRST —TO— ARRIVE
ARITHMETIC LESSON NO. 1
Freight Shipments + Routing by Steamer = Good Service
F. S. FARQUAR, Freight Agent Petaluma, Cal.
Don't Fail to Specify Routing
H. S. GRAHAM, Asstist. Gen'l. Frt. Agt. Petaluma, Cal.
E. H. MAGGARD, General Manager, Petaluma, Cal.

The Petaluma & Santa Rosa Railroad Company. The railway company was incorporated in 1903, but initial rapid growth was stunted by the 1906 earthquake, which severely damaged downtown Santa Rosa. Petaluma was left relatively intact. After financial problems, it was organized as the Petaluma & Santa Rosa Railroad Company in 1918, with George P. McNear as a founding member. With the connection between steamer ships and the Petaluma & Santa Rosa Railroad, the company could provide overnight shipping from San Francisco to Sebastopol. (Courtesy Lew Baer.)

Steamer Paddle Boats. This image shows the steamer *Gold* at Steamer's Landing in the McNear Channel. In 1950, her sister ship, the steamer *Petaluma*, made the last regular run of any commercial stern-wheeler not only in Petaluma, but in all of California. (Courtesy Lew Baer.)

INITIAL RAILROAD DEPOT. This postcard, mailed in 1913, shows the San Francisco & North Pacific Railroad depot, built in 1871 by Col. Peter Donahue on Lakeville Street between Washington and D Streets. Note the horse-drawn carriages to the right. Donahue was a tycoon who made his money by establishing the first foundry, iron molding, print press, and quartz mill in San Francisco, profiting from the Gold Rush. He originally intended for Petaluma to be the terminus. When Petaluma city officials would not let him build tracks for his railroad down the middle of Main Street, Donahue decided to create his own town and terminus eight miles downstream, along the eastern bank of the river. By 1884, he extended his line from Petaluma to Tiburon via San Rafael and moved his town's buildings by barge to the new terminus. The expansion of the railroad brought more population to Sonoma County. By 1880, landlocked Santa Rosa had grown to be more populous than Petaluma (3,616 versus 3,326) as the transportation lines fueled growth. (Courtesy Lew Baer.)

THE NORTHWESTERN PACIFIC DEPOT. Designed by D.J. Patterson, a Southern Pacific Railroad staff architect, this mission revival depot was dedicated on April 24, 1914, replacing the 1871 depot, which was moved to the back lot and repurposed as a freight depot. Patterson's other architectural designs include the Union Pacific Station in Salt Lake City and the Union Station in Seattle. The Petaluma depot was built primarily by local subcontractors, with Schluckebier providing the hardware, Van Bebber Brothers the ironwork, and Camm & Hedges the lumber and millwork. At the time this depot was built, the Northwestern Pacific Railroad ran from Tiburon through Petaluma and Santa Rosa to Cloverdale, with a spur to Guerneville. The back of the postcard above reads, "This is the Depot you will land at in Petaluma."

Railroads in Petaluma History. The first railroad built in Petaluma and reportedly the third railroad built in the state of California was the Petaluma & Haystack Railroad in 1864 (five years prior to the transcontinental railroad), which ran two and a half miles down Second Street from B Street along the west bank of the Petaluma Creek to Haystack Landing, a steamboat terminus in the early years. The "Ferry Boat King," Charles Minturn, built the line and purchased a small steam locomotive and created a monopoly on bringing passengers to and from Petaluma. In 1866, there was a disastrous explosion of the engine, which killed several people. For the remaining years of its existence, mules pulled the railroad cars to and from town. The San Francisco & North Pacific Railroad and the Petaluma & Santa Rosa Railroad (P&SR) connected Petaluma with destinations north and south. Both were eventually acquired by the Northwestern Pacific Railroad (NWP). As automobiles became a viable mode of transportation, there were fewer passengers on trains, and in 1932, the P&SR curtailed passenger service. This image shows the NWP No. 182 in Petaluma.

Three

THE HEART OF PETALUMA

DOWNTOWN

DOWNTOWN PETALUMA. By the 1870s, Petaluma had become an important commercial and shipping center. This postcard is of Main Street, called the "Heart of Petaluma" by the Petaluma *Argus-Courier* in 1958, looking south from Washington Street. On the left is Scott's Hardware Store, one of Petaluma's earliest retailers. Main Street was renamed Petaluma Boulevard in 1958. The buildings on the east side of Main Street were used for both industrial and retail purposes. The rear of the buildings faced the waterfront, providing access to river and rail transportation. (Courtesy Craig Blackstone.)

EARLY UPPER AND LOWER MAIN STREET. A view of Main Street looking south at the Washington Street intersection. The building on the right is the old Sonoma County Bank building with the Derby Block across the street. The above postcard provides a glimpse into what was originally the center of town, the intersection of Main Street and Washington Street. Below is a postcard from the 1910s with a view looking north at Center Park and Main Street. In the middle of the postcard is a view of the landmark Masonic Lodge building with the original clock tower. The Petaluma Masonic Hall Association built the three-story High Victorian Italianate–style building in 1882. The clock tower was built by Seth Thomas in Connecticut and assumed to have been shipped around Cape Horn to Petaluma.

New Clock Tower. The wooden tower began to deteriorate and was replaced in 1934 with this new tower with copper siding. The original clockwork remained. The clock tower on the Masonic Lodge building is one of Petaluma's most iconic downtown landmarks. The clock tower was not original to the building; it was added after Petalumans wanted a symbol of prosperity and raised the funds for it. The City of Petaluma would eventually own this iconic clock tower. (Courtesy Petaluma Museum.)

Main Street, 1950s. A view of Main Street looking north with the Masonic Lodge building with the clock tower on the immediate left. The stunning Neoclassical-style bank building, also on the left, was completed in 1928 by the American Trust Company, formerly the Mercantile Trust Company and the Petaluma National Bank. American Trust Company merged with the Wells Fargo Bank in 1960. The site was formerly known as the Whitney Block.

MAIN STREET, FROM WESTERN AVENUE, 1900S. This postcard mailed in 1910 provides a view of Main Street from Western Avenue. The building on the northeast corner is Petaluma National Bank, erected in 1903 and torn down in 1926 to make room for the American Trust Company bank structure. Next to the bank is the Odd Fellows building, completed in 1871.

KENTUCKY STREET AND WESTERN AVENUE, 1940S. This is a view looking north along Kentucky Street from Western Avenue. The Leader department store building was erected in 1941 by Mose Goldman. The Streamline Moderne architectural style was characterized by its aerodynamic features and was a popular design for commercial buildings at the time. In 1946, the Carithers Company bought the Leader building, and the structure went on to serve several other large stores. On the right is the Price Building, erected in 1910, with Antlers Pharmacy on the ground floor.

KENTUCKY STREET ABOVE WASHINGTON STREET, 1910S. The Herold Building, identified by its round turret constructed in 1899 on the corner of Kentucky and Washington Streets, replaced the Washington Stable and Livery. The two-story Queen Anne–style commercial building was constructed for Angela Canepa, a recent widow. In 1908, Cyrus Young and Harry Herold moved their drugstore to this location. In 1913, Herold became the sole owner. The vacant lot on the right of the postcard is where the Hotel Petaluma was built in 1924. (Courtesy Craig Blackstone.)

KENTUCKY STREET AND WASHINGTON STREET, 1900S. This postcard mailed in 1908 provides a view looking south along Kentucky Street from the corner of Washington Street. On the far right is part of the Herold Building, where one of the bay windows angles out and the other one is curved. The Healey Building, constructed in 1904, is the second building from the right. The fourth building from the right is the Opera House, erected in 1870.

Early Washington Street. This view of Washington Street is looking west around 1910 toward the intersection with Main Street. On the right is the Peek & Wilson Cash Grocers, with an advertisement of "Brooder House Stoves" and the Petaluma Rooming House next door.

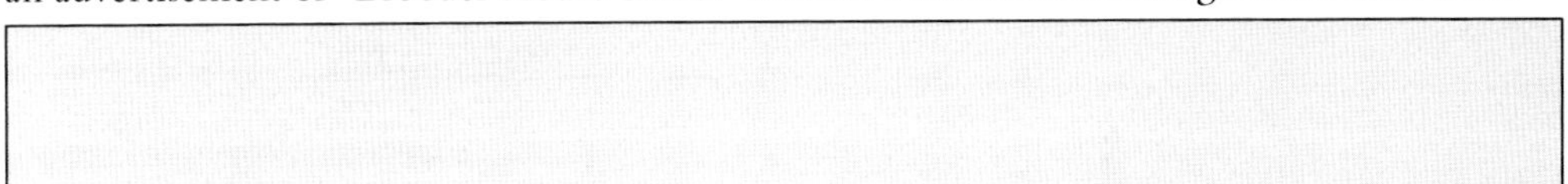

Washington Bridge and Upper Main Street. This postcard from the early 1900s is of the first Washington Street Bridge. The set of buildings at the bottom center, before crossing the swing bridge, included the Schlukebier Hardware Company's wagon and buggy sales office. The company's hardware store was on Main Street. The McCune Block is on the right after crossing the bridge and was torn down in 1962. The lot stayed vacant, and the parcel was used in widening Washington Street in 1969. (Courtesy Sonoma County Library.)

Iron Storefronts on Western Avenue. One of Petaluma's most significant architectural contributions is the row of buildings with cast-iron facades on Western Avenue between Main and Kentucky Streets. The Italianate-style iron fronts of these 1880s structures grace the entire block on the south side of the street and were erroneously presumed to be fire-resistant. The pieces were manufactured in Bay Area foundries and shipped to Petaluma to be assembled and bolted to the brick walls. (Courtesy Craig Blackstone.)

Petaluma Historic Commercial District. Downtown Petaluma has an expansive and well-preserved collection of historic commercial buildings with different architectural styles. Petaluma had minimal damage from the 1906 earthquake and also escaped the downtown redevelopment trend of the 1960s, resulting in minimal loss of historic structures. In 1995, the Petaluma Commercial District was listed in the National Register of Historic Places. This postcard, sent in 1955, reads, "You can see the Main St. of Petaluma. It's quite a nice little town."

PETALUMA'S GROWTH AND DEVELOPMENT. In 1950, Petaluma had around 10,000 people and added 4,000 a decade later. After 1960, with the completion of Highway 101, there was more rapid growth; the population was 24,000 by 1970. The growth was of great concern for Petaluma residents, which resulted in a controversial decision in 1972. The first voter-approved growth control initiative in California allowed the City of Petaluma to approve a maximum of 500 new home units per year, which was half of the previous year's total.

Four

The Commercial Metropolis of Sonoma County

Early Industry

Commerce and Industry. The river was a strategic asset in the early years of the town of Petaluma, affording transportation to San Francisco, Sacramento, and other destinations, which encouraged industrial growth. This postcard, postmarked 1911, shows the Carlson-Currier Silk Mill and the Nolan and Earl Shoe Factory. The *Illustrated Atlas of Sonoma County*, published in 1897, proclaimed that by "common consent" Petaluma had been "accorded the title of 'The Commercial Metropolis of Sonoma County.' "

EARLY INDUSTRIES. This postcard, postmarked in 1913, showcases poultry farms and fruit farms, two major industries in Petaluma. Four decades earlier, in the 1870s, Petaluma had 27 saloons, 11 blacksmith and wagon-making shops, 10 shoe shops, 7 hotels, 7 livery stables, 6 carpentry shops, 4 cabinetmakers, 3 lumber yards, 3 tin shops, 3 tanneries, 2 banks, 2 breweries, 2 flour mills, and 1 of each of the following: candy factory, glove factory, marble works, and pottery works. In 1870, annual exports from Petaluma included 75,000 dozen eggs, 6,000 poultry, 12,000 quail, 9,000 pounds of hay, 3,000 pounds of grain, 200,000 sacks of potatoes, and 40,000 boxes of fruit, as reported in the *Illustrated Atlas of Sonoma County.* This brought prosperity and growth to town; Petaluma was incorporated in 1858 and had a population of 1,505 in 1860. By the 1880 census, the population had more than doubled to 3,326.

Dairy Farms. As with many other industries, dairy in Petaluma evolved with technology and industrialization. The image above shows a bucolic scene, with cows grazing in open pasture. During the post–Gold Rush years, as California population boomed, Petaluma farmers produced and exported dairy products. The 1877 *Historical and Descriptive Sketch of Sonoma County* reported that annual exports from Petaluma included 3.5 million pounds of butter, 750,000 pounds of cheese, and 1,500 head of cattle. (Courtesy Craig Blackstone.)

Creameries. In 1913, a total of 33 Sonoma and Marin County dairy farmers, organized by Silvio Gambonini, banded together to establish the Petaluma Cooperative Creamery for producing and marketing premium butter. This postcard is of the first churn room with butter churns at the Western Avenue facility. In 1916, the cooperative adopted the "Clover" brand name and, over time, also sold milk, cottage cheese, and other dairy products. (Courtesy Petaluma Museum.)

Wagons and Buggies. Petaluma was a major producer of wagons and buggies in the state of California. This postcard shows the Schluckebier Hardware Company, just east of the Washington Street Bridge, advertising wagons and buggies. The first such company in Petaluma was William Zartman & Company, Carriage and Wagonmakers, established in 1852 first on Main Street and later at the corner of Western Avenue and Howard Street. The Zartman company advertised in the 1884 *Petaluma City Directory* that it "will fill all orders for Buggies, Family Carriages, Side and End-Spring Ranch Wagons, All Styles Two-Wheeled Vehicles, etc." with a "good assortment Constantly on Hand." More industries were established in Petaluma, as it was the major transportation hub of the region. (Courtesy Petaluma Museum.)

LUMBER. One of the earliest large imports to Petaluma was lumber, arriving first via wagon and then by train from the forests of Sonoma County and points farther north. Humboldt redwood, Oregon pine, and cedar were also shipped upriver from San Francisco. This image shows lumber being unloaded in Petaluma from a schooner. (Courtesy Petaluma Museum.)

MILLWORK. Camm & Hedges, located across the street from the Golden Eagle Mill, was an early lumber and planing mill. In 1897, the *Illustrated Atlas of Sonoma County* reported "the company's mill and yards cover an area of one entire block . . . the splendid planing mill is equipped with the latest improved planing, sawing, and other machinery operated by a twenty-five horsepower engine, and capable of turning out the finest grade of work in mouldings, doors, and windows—in fact, all kinds of millwork and finished building material of every description." (Courtesy Sonoma County Library.)

FEED AND STORAGE. John A. McNear was enticed to relocate to Petaluma by his father-in-law, George B. Williams, who had built the American and Washington Hotels in town. McNear and his bride of two years, Clarinda "Clara" Damsen Williams, came west in 1856. John was 23 years old and first started in the livery stable and hay yard business. He branched out into money lending, a shipping enterprise on the river, and a large warehouse in 1864 to store, sell, and ship grain, flour, and hay. He also turned to milling, and in 1876, at the age of 19, his son George P. McNear took over the mill, eventually incorporating it into the George P. McNear Company in 1913. A new large mill was built in 1903 by McNear on Main Street at B Street along the river to facilitate sales and shipping. The image on this page (postmarked 1910) shows a schooner at the McNear dock at the McNear Feed Mill. The McNear family played a large role in the development of Petaluma, including donating land for McNear Park and McNear School.

FARM SUPPLIES. As the poultry and dairy industries grew in Petaluma in the late 1800s, so did supportive businesses, including feed stores. In addition to George P. McNear, many other competing companies emerged: Coulson, Vonsen, Parker & Gordon, and R.O. Shelling, to name a few. In 1921, Marvin Hunt and Carl Behrens, former employees at McNear's Mill, started their own business and built a mill along the river at First and C Streets. The waterfront scene above (postmarked 1931) shows the Hunt & Behrens warehouse and a schooner loaded with cargo. The image below was taken looking north across the turning basin, with Hunt & Behrens on the left and the Golden Eagle Mill on the right. (Below, courtesy Petaluma Museum.)

The First Bank in Sonoma County. The first bank between San Francisco and Oregon was established in Petaluma in 1865 by Isaak Wickersham. His private banking business constructed the first bank building in Sonoma County in 1868. In 1874, the bank was granted a charter as one of only 10 national "gold" banks, with nine located in California. This allowed the First National Gold Bank of Petaluma to issue legal paper currency backed by gold. This postcard shows the Bank of Sonoma County to the right, on the northwest corner of Washington and Main Streets. (Courtesy Sonoma County Library.)

The Banking Industry. In 1866, John A. McNear, who had been successful lending money, led a group of citizens to establish the Bank of Sonoma County with a capital stock of $100,000. As a regional commercial hub, Petaluma was naturally also a regional banking and finance hub. This postcard (postmarked 1950) shows a bank at left, on the corner of Main Street and Western Avenue, originally built by the American Trust Company in 1928.

Downtown Businesses. Petaluma had a thriving downtown, including the sale of staples for business and home as well as luxury items. The above postcard shows Morrow's confections and ice-cream truck in front, with Annie Morrow as the likely driver, advertising ice cream, candies, and peanuts. In 1860, a soda works established by B.F. Connolly advertised "soda, sarsaparilla, and champaigne cider." A cigar factory was opened in 1871, with A. Horstman as proprietor. There were also hotels, groceries, banks, barbershops, and other retail businesses. The image below shows the interior of Volpi's grocery store at Kentucky and Washington Streets. (Both, courtesy Petaluma Museum.)

SILK MANUFACTURING. In 1892, San Francisco architect Charles Havens designed this two-story industrial brick building reminiscent of the Victorian New England textile mills for the Carlson-Currier Silk Manufacturing Company. The land had been purchased from local business entrepreneur John A. McNear, who was eager to support local manufacturing endeavors. Petaluma was at the forefront of California's effort in developing sericulture (silk farming) with the only silk mill west of the Mississippi River. (Courtesy Petaluma Museum.)

SILK MILL DYEING ROOM. The cultivation of silkworms in California was temporary and unsuccessful. The Carlson-Currier Company turned to importing raw silk from China, Japan, and Italy for processing instead. The original building included a silk vault, boiler plant, and a dye house. This postcard is of the interior of the "dyeing department," a one-story building used for coloring the silk, located to the back of the main building, with a loading dock to Wilson Street. (Courtesy Petaluma Museum.)

BELDING-HEMINGWAY-CORTICELLI. The Belding brothers, together with Hemingway and Corticelli, purchased the mill in 1917 and continued with the production of silk thread and other sewing products. In 1922, construction of the second tower and wing was completed, doubling the size of the structure with styling similar to the original building. This interior postcard of the stretchers was done by Petaluma's Decker Studio. The Deckers were married professional photographers who owned one of the largest studios in the area.

SUNSET LINE & TWINE COMPANY. This card was postmarked in 1908. Silk manufacturing ceased in 1929, but the mill continued with the production of synthetic and other natural materials. In 1940, the Sunset Line & Twine Company purchased the building and became known for the production of fishing lines and specialized materials for specific industries, including the Apollo space program. The Georgia Colonial Revival–style building was placed in the National Register of Historic Places in 1986.

Flour Mills. The first flour mill in Petaluma was the Occidental Mill on Grey Street. The Golden Eagle Milling Company, shown in this image (postmarked 1912), was founded in 1885, and in the Scudder's *Petaluma City Directory* of 1895, the company boasted that its flour was "the strongest and whitest" and "the product of home industry." In the same advertisement, the company promoted its other products: hay, straw, lime, cement, salt, chicken feed, bale rope, twine, grain bags, wood, and coal.

Grain Elevators. Industrial advances brought new technology to commerce in Petaluma. In 1937, the Poultry Producers Cooperative of Central California (PPCCC) built this 110-foot structure on the east side of the Petaluma River just north of Washington Street. The grain elevator was just one aspect of the PPCCC's plant. At its peak in 1949, this facility employed 415 workers, including 200 women candlers processing 4.5 million eggs per week.

OIL WELLS. An advertisement in the *Santa Rosa Republican* on September 9, 1909, seeking investment for the Bonita Oil Company boasted, "Oil Struck! Gas Struck! At Sonoma Valley's New Oil Fields." Another article on October 12, 1909, states that the Petaluma Home Company was poised to begin digging its first well, and Bonita was ready for its second. The Petaluma and Ramona oil companies also dug wells. The wells were primarily located in east Petaluma, including on the Riebli, Ducker, Pattochi, and Meacham properties. Oil production diminished as it became cheaper to produce from more plentiful fields such as in Kern County. However, oil wells in Petaluma continued producing until about 1950. (Both, courtesy Petaluma Museum.)

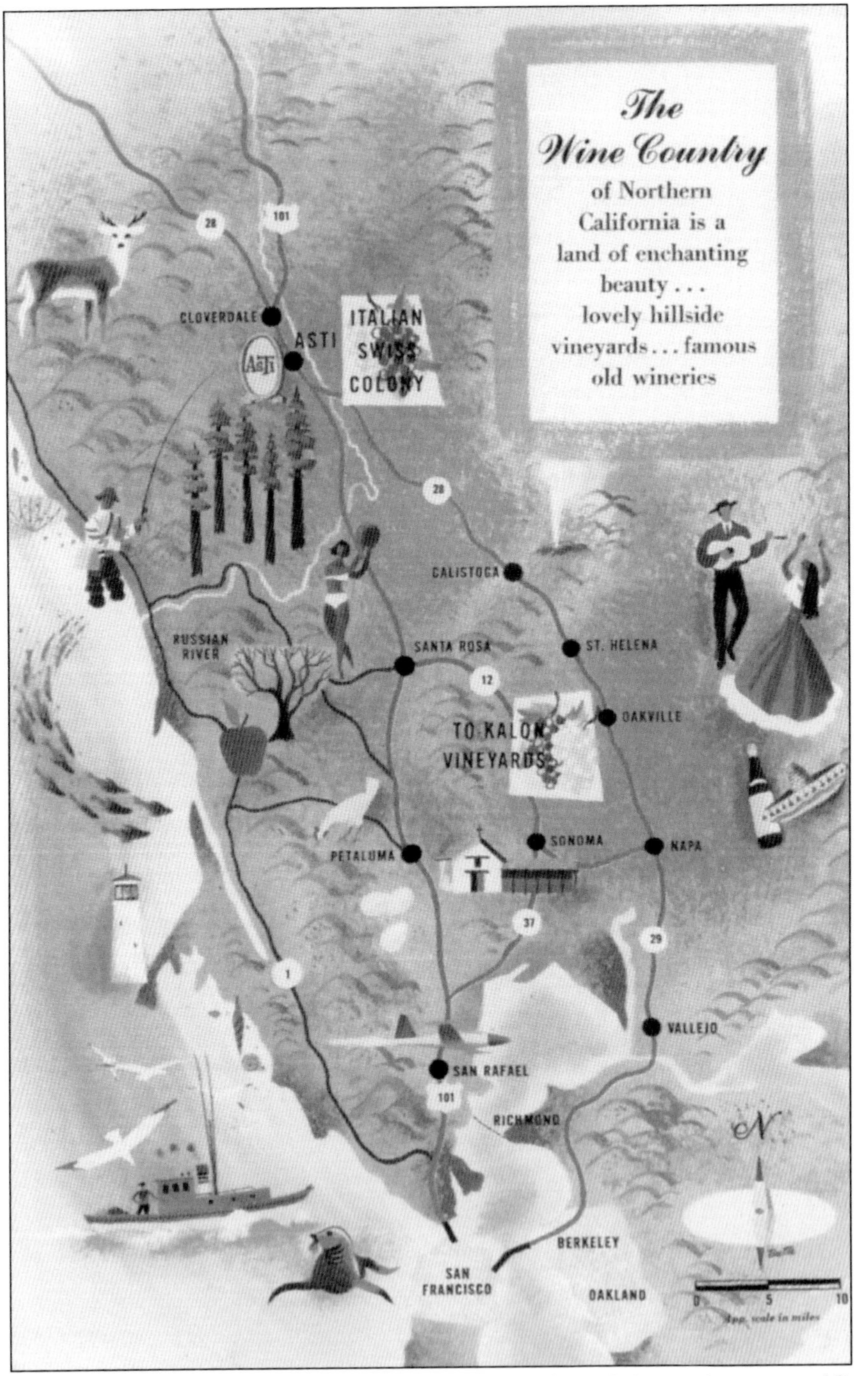

PIONEER WINERIES. In the mid-1800s, a substantial number of vineyards were established in the Lakeville area, and by the early 1900s, the region boasted 1,000 acres of vines. European immigrants settling in the Petaluma area fueled the demand for local wine production. The climate and soil conditions made grape growing feasible. Grapes and wine could also be transported from Petaluma along the waterway to San Francisco and other locations. The early Petaluma wineries did not survive Prohibition.

Lachman & Jacobi Winery. One of the largest California wineries in 1904, Lachman & Jacobi was headquartered in San Francisco. The 1906 earthquake destroyed its plant, which led the company to rebuild in Petaluma. The winery purchased 10 acres along the railroad tracks of the Northwestern Pacific Railroad at the northwest corner of Lakeville and Washington Streets and constructed eight separate buildings. The reinforced cement tanks stored four million gallons of wine and half a million gallons of brandy. Sonoma County wineries could transport their wine to Petaluma for storing or blending before being shipped to San Francisco. The plant was sold to the National Ice Company in 1918, before Prohibition. The buildings were torn down in 1973. (Both, courtesy Gail Unzelman.)

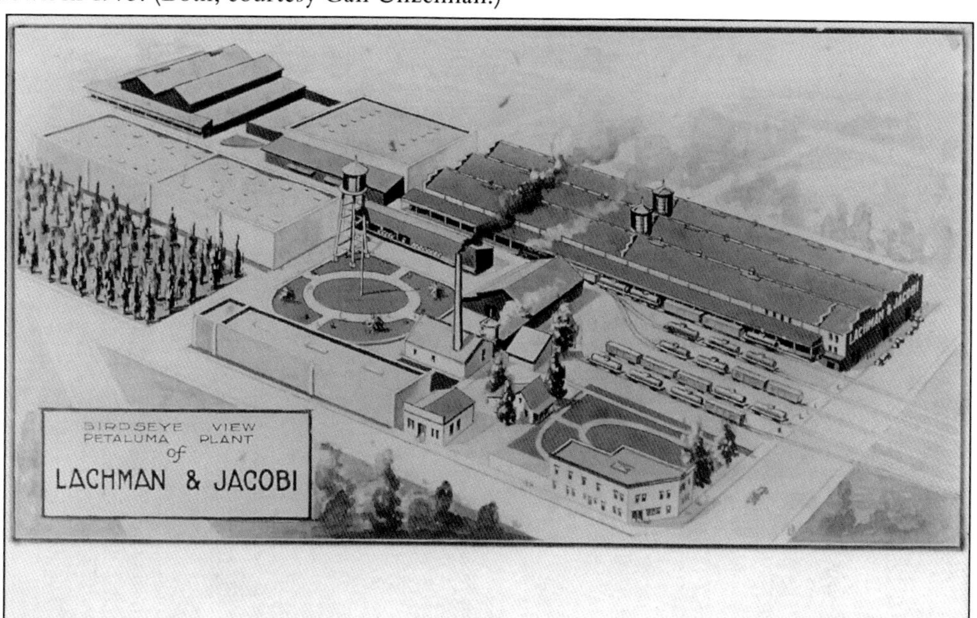

U.S. BREWERY. The first brewery in Sonoma County was in Petaluma. The Petaluma Brewery opened in 1855 and was located on Main Street, with a beer garden and hanging arbors. George Griess immigrated to Petaluma from France in 1870 and joined Charles Mitchell in operating the Sonoma Brewery. A decade later, he established the U.S. Brewery, pictured here on Upham Street near Bodega Avenue, which he operated until his death in 1914. Petaluma was a significant and successful transportation hub that supported diverse industries, including luxury goods for local consumption and export. (Courtesy Sonoma County Library.)

Five

The Largest Poultry Center on Earth

Chickens and Eggs

Petaluma Poultry. From approximately 1890 to 1960, poultry was the primary industry in Petaluma. The development of successful incubators and brooders propelled the town to the forefront of chicken and egg production. The chamber of commerce published a pamphlet in 1909 promoting Petaluma as "the Largest Poultry Center on Earth" and included information to entice "homeseekers" to move to town. And many did—the population of Petaluma nearly doubled between 1900 and 1920, growing from 3,871 to 6,226.

FAMILY CHICKEN RANCHES. Conditions in Petaluma were ideal for chicken ranches and egg production, with a mild year-round climate, sandy loam soil, and the river and railroad providing access to outside markets. In the early years, Petaluma families typically raised their own chickens for meat and eggs and sold surplus to port destinations such as San Francisco. There were no ranches or farms that focused exclusively on chickens until the 1880s. By the turn of the century, family chicken ranches proliferated in Petaluma. For approximately $4,000, one could purchase land and improvements and livestock to create a poultry farm, with a profit of $1 per year per hen, which allowed a family to live comfortably. Reportedly in 1904, nine-tenths of Petaluma residents were raising poultry, and related industries in town were thriving.

LIFE ON THE RANCH. By all reports, chicken ranching was hard work. Eggs had to be gathered daily, a task often performed by children, and had to be candled for quality and hand-cleaned for sale. Eggs in early incubators needed to be turned two to three times a day. Chicks had to be "sexed" to separate the cockerels (juvenile males) from the pullets (juvenile females). Upon maturity, hens were generally put in colony houses, and roosters were sold for meat.

RELATED WORK. Eggs had to be packaged carefully to minimize breakage and were shipped with the little end down. Eggs and chickens needed to be transported to town for sale, and feed needed to be brought back to the ranch. Chicken droppings required mucking and could be sold as fertilizer. As the poultry industry evolved, chickens also needed vaccinations and to have their beaks and wings clipped.

The Petaluma Incubator. The 1879 development in Petaluma of the first viable commercial egg incubator, which could maintain a temperature of 103 degrees for three weeks to hatch eggs while not taking a hen out of egg production, revolutionized the industry. Lyman Byce took full credit for inventing and perfecting the incubator, but historians believe Petaluma dentist Isaac Dias also deserves credit. The two were initially partners, but Dias died in 1884. This postcard, sent in 1910, reads, "This is a great place for hatching little chickens. The big hatcheries are open the year around."

Promoting Incubators. Lyman Byce promoted his Petaluma Incubator far and wide for decades by attending expositions and fairs, where it won many awards. He was a masterful marketer and developed catalogs replete with unsubstantiated claims and grandiose self-promotion. Another publicity stunt was hatching exotic eggs, such as ostrich eggs. Nevertheless, the product was solid. By 1883, the Petaluma Incubator Company had sold 200 units, mostly to local family-owned farms, and by 1897, more than 15,000 incubators had been sold to a much broader world market.

Need for Brooders. Once incubators became a reliable means of hatching chickens, the baby chicks had to be kept warm for their first three weeks in order to survive. Without a brooding mother hen, an artificial way had to be devised. Christopher Nisson, who arrived in California from Denmark in 1868 at the age of 19, had his own ranch by 1880 and purchased a new incubator from the Petaluma Incubator Company. Inspired, he developed the first-known mechanical brooder, to do what in nature is performed by mother hens. As the images above and below illustrate, brooders had many designs and evolved over the years. The card below is postmarked 1921.

TECHNOLOGY EVOLVES. Competition, demand, and technological advances such as electricity, which serviced incubators by 1908, fueled innovation in the poultry industry, especially as ranches and hatcheries scaled up production. Petaluma, as the emerging center of the poultry industry in the nation, was home to much of this innovation. Local chicken ranchers tinkered and developed improvements on existing incubators and brooders. While competing incubators were developed and manufactured in Petaluma and elsewhere, the successful commercial industry started in Petaluma spawned further poultry innovations such as advanced brooders and mechanical contraptions to wash eggs clean. The postcards on this page illustrate how technologies and practices evolved to support the poultry industry, which was growing in numbers of farms as well as scale. The card above reads, "This is great chicken country. All kinds. Broilers, Squabs and old hens." The image below is of Danger's Ranch.

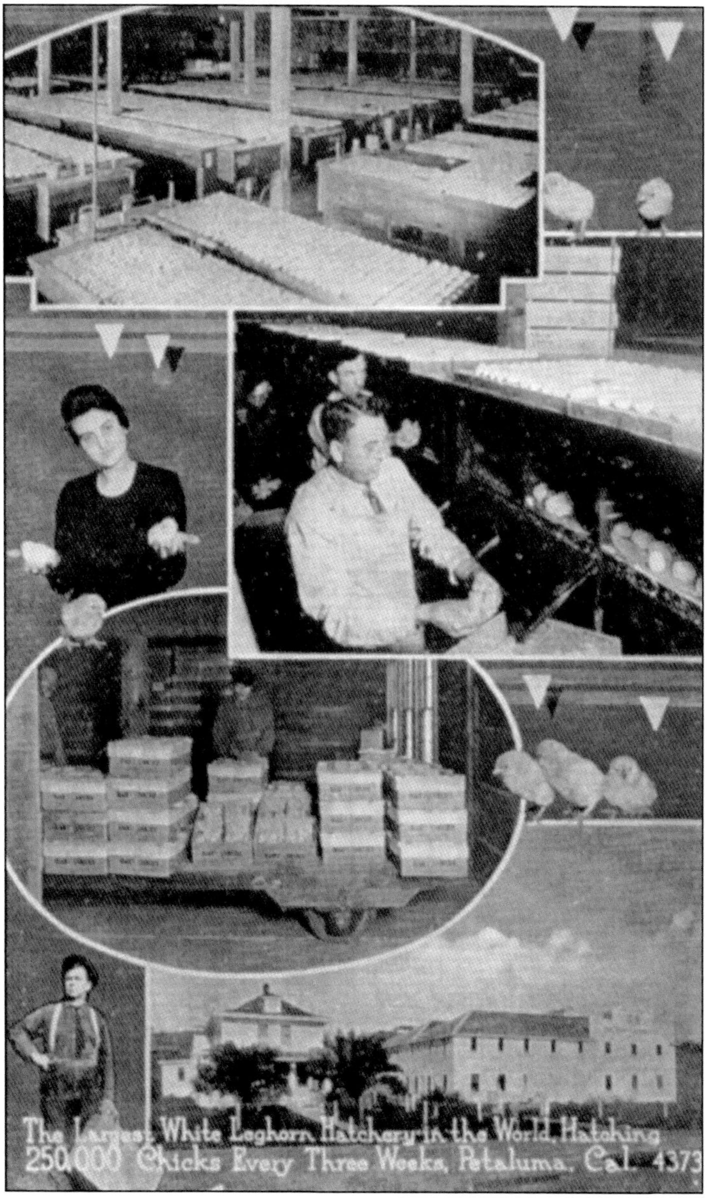

An Industry Emerges. The widespread use of the egg incubator thrust Petaluma into the national and international markets. These new technologies greatly increased productivity on chicken farms. Supportive industries emerged in Petaluma, including poultry feed, packaging, refrigeration, shipping, and poultry science. In 1903, recognizing the importance of the poultry industry centered in Petaluma, the State of California Legislature appropriated $5,000 to establish the California Poultry Experiment Station in Petaluma, on land given by George P. McNear. The station hired scientists who primarily came from Cornell University, the nation's foremost poultry science school at the time, to study poultry nutrition, pathology, incubation, brooding, and parasitology. In 1915, the newly created University of California Extension began serving Petaluma, and by 1926, the university assigned a full-time poultry pathologist to the Livestock and Poultry Pathology Laboratory, the world's only institute devoted solely to the study of poultry pathology and research for treatments and cures, located on F Street.

The Chicken Pharmacy. The poultry industry was so widespread in Petaluma that a pharmacy focused exclusively on chickens opened in 1923 at 215 Main Street, then moved to 176 Main Street, pictured here. Started by James Davis, the Chicken Pharmacy truthfully boasted that it was "the only store of its kind in the world," as it sold "medicines and remedies for fowls only." The pharmacy was featured in the February 1939 issue of *National Geographic* and in *Ripley's Believe it or Not.*

Transporting Chickens and Eggs. In the early days, live chickens and eggs were transported by wagon to town, and surplus was shipped downriver to San Francisco or other ports furnishing the gold miners, like Sacramento. Once it was understood that chicks could survive for 48 hours without food or water, hatchlings were shipped. In 1918, the US Post Office accepted baby chicks into their transit system, thus expediting shipment.

THE THOMAS RANCH. The W.R. Thomas Poultry Ranch, working with the White Hatchery, was one of the many successful operations in Petaluma after the turn of the 19th century. This image shows the stately and proud ranch owner, along with his flock of White Leghorns, who became the hens of choice at Petaluma chicken ranches due to their high egg productivity. The back of the card enumerates egg productivity for one month, February 1912, when chickens at the large ranch produced 16,485 eggs. The Thomas Poultry Ranch and other similar operations illustrate how the poultry industry was evolving from smaller family farms to larger, more industrial pursuits.

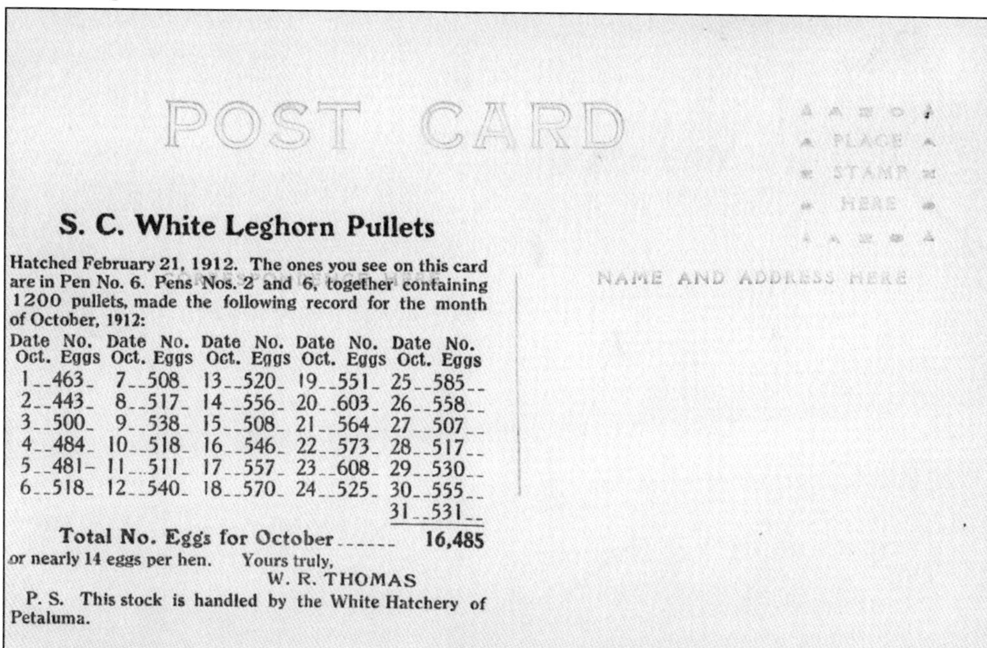
POST CARD

PLACE STAMP HERE

NAME AND ADDRESS HERE

S. C. White Leghorn Pullets

Hatched February 21, 1912. The ones you see on this card are in Pen No. 6. Pens Nos. 2 and 6, together containing 1200 pullets, made the following record for the month of October, 1912:

Date Oct.	No. Eggs	Date Oct.	No. Eggs	Date Oct.	No. Eggs	Date Oct.	No. Eggs	Date Oct.	No. Eggs
1	463	7	508	13	520	19	551	25	585
2	443	8	517	14	556	20	603	26	558
3	500	9	538	15	508	21	564	27	507
4	484	10	518	16	546	22	573	28	517
5	481	11	511	17	557	23	608	29	530
6	518	12	540	18	570	24	525	30	555
								31	531

Total No. Eggs for October 16,485

or nearly 14 eggs per hen. Yours truly,

W. R. THOMAS

P. S. This stock is handled by the White Hatchery of Petaluma.

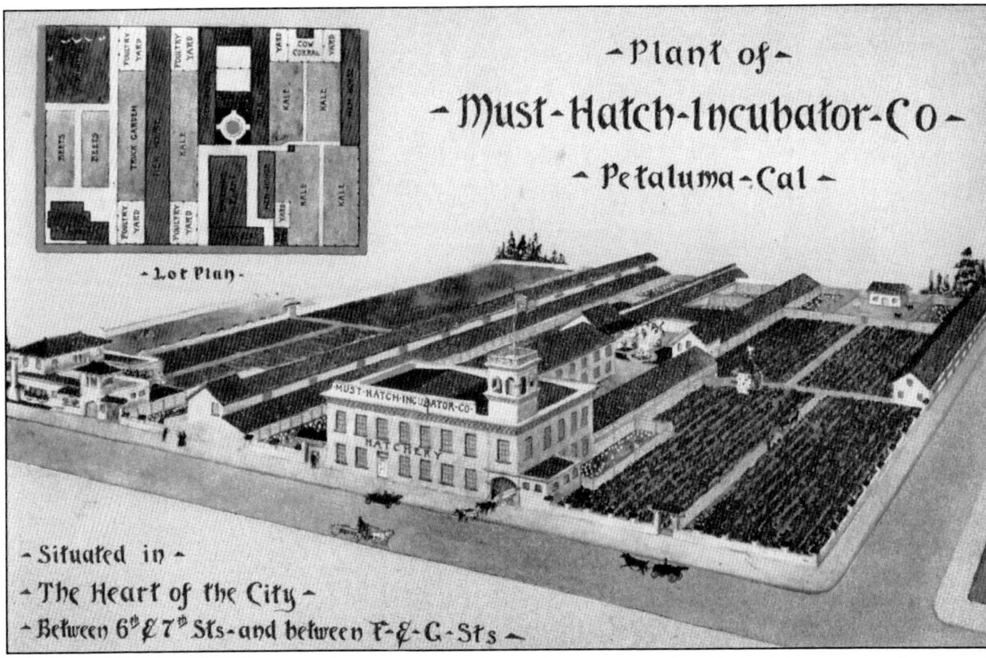

THE INDUSTRY GROWS. The first commercial egg hatchery in the United States was developed by Christopher Nisson, a Danish immigrant, at his Two-Rock ranch. Nisson is credited with industry innovations, including mechanical brooders and the widely used "colony house," which kept chickens on a raised platform with a slotted floor that could be moved when the droppings were thick on the ground, thus easing clean up. In 1898, he started the Pioneer Hatchery at 418 Sixth Street. Other Petalumans followed Nisson's lead and began devoting farms to egg production. Nisson's sons Jack and Eric eventually took over the Pioneer Hatchery, growing it to be one of the largest hatcheries in the country, with a capacity of 20,000 eggs in 1910 and 500,000 in 1940. These images show the front and back of a postcard advertising the Must Hatch Incubator Company.

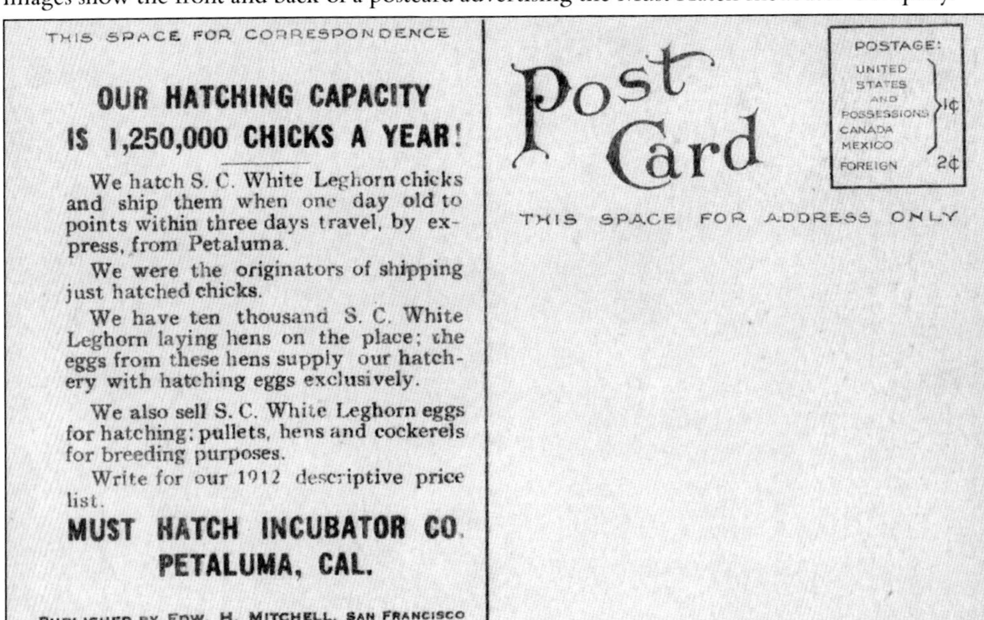

CHICKEN HATCHERIES. The Pioneer Hatchery may have been the first commercial hatchery in Petaluma and the nation, but many more opened up in town. The Must Hatch Incubator Company was founded in 1898 by Alphonse Bourke, who also opened a hatchery on Seventh Street in 1910. The first hatchery was destroyed by fire in 1923. When rebuilt in 1927 at 401 Seventh Street, with Brainerd Jones as the architect, the Must Hatch Incubator Company claimed to be the "World's Largest Hatchery," with the tagline "A Greater Birthplace for a Greater Chick." At its peak, the hatchery employed 500 workers and hatched a maximum of 1.8 million chicks daily. The company, headed by president and general manager Leo Bourke, son of the founder, also manufactured and sold incubators and brooders. The card below is an advertisement sent to "Post Office Box Holder, Sonoma, Calif." in 1931. (Right, courtesy Lew Baer.)

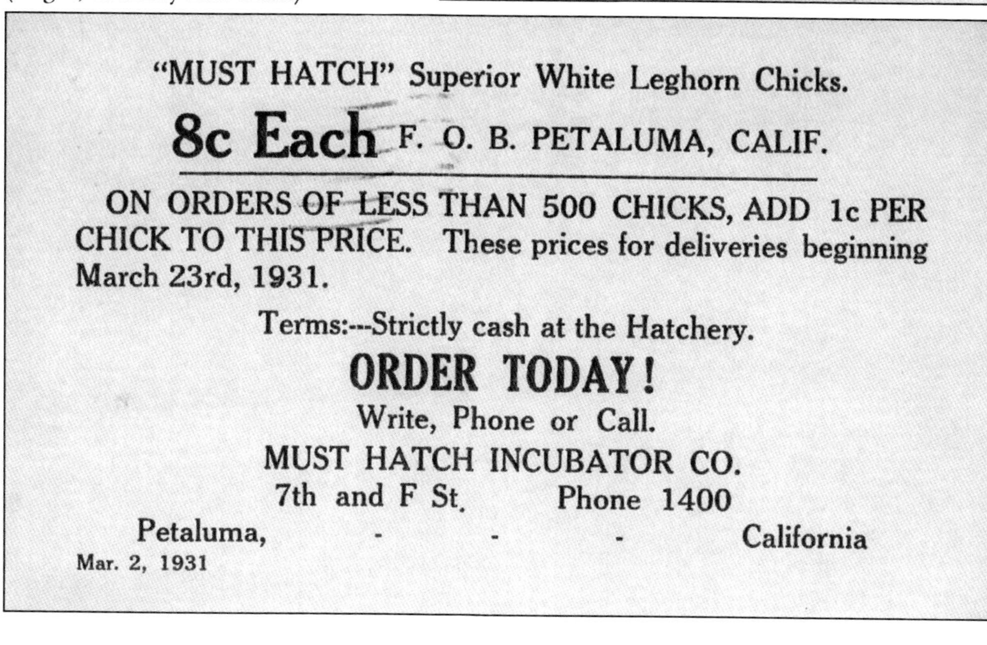
"MUST HATCH" Superior White Leghorn Chicks.

8c Each F. O. B. PETALUMA, CALIF.

ON ORDERS OF LESS THAN 500 CHICKS, ADD 1c PER CHICK TO THIS PRICE. These prices for deliveries beginning March 23rd, 1931.

Terms:---Strictly cash at the Hatchery.

ORDER TODAY!

Write, Phone or Call.

MUST HATCH INCUBATOR CO.

7th and F St. Phone 1400

Petaluma, - - - California

Mar. 2, 1931

The Proliferation of Petaluma Poultry. As the poultry industry continued to grow and flourish in Petaluma, more attention was paid to the science behind maximizing output and, therefore, profit. Selective breeding, "sexing" chicks to separate the pullets from the cockerels, culling nonproductive hens, and grading eggs for quality took on new importance. Egg laying, candling, and chicken sexing competitions were held with prizes widely publicized. Further avian science was encouraged—and funded by the federal and state governments—in developing scientifically balanced feed, disease control, forced molt experiments, genetic studies, egg storage, and shipping practices. Poultry production expanded to include other birds, notably turkeys. The Poehlmann Hatchery, founded in 1918 by Frank and Bertha Poehlmann, pioneered turkey incubation starting in 1928. Their hatchery was initially located at 15 Kent Street but moved to a new building at 620 Main Street, on the site of a former livery stable.

The Chicken and Egg Capitol. By the 1890s, there were six egg hatcheries operating in Petaluma, and in 1905, nearly 46 million eggs were shipped from the town. By the 1920s, the number of hatcheries grew to about two dozen. That same year, Petaluma shipped out an estimated 264 million eggs, making the town and surrounding farms the largest poultry producing region in America. In 1926, Petaluma's population was approximately 7,000, and chicken farms numbered about 2,000, with an average of seven acres each. In 1940, about seven million baby chicks and turkeys were shipped from Petaluma. The town seemed justified in calling itself the chicken and egg capital of the world. (Above, courtesy Petaluma Museum.)

LARGE-SCALE EGG PRODUCTION. Petaluma was provisioning a growing market. In 1910, per capita egg consumption in the United States exceeded 300 eggs per person, and the population was on the rise. During World War II, when meat was rationed, the demand for eggs increased, and in 1945, egg consumption reached 397 eggs per capita. Petaluma eggs were shipped nationwide, but California was the biggest market. In 1940, Petaluma produced 32 percent of California's eggs. The images on this page depict the interiors of large-scale egg packaging (above, Nye and Nisson) and hatchery (below, the Petaluma Hatchery) enterprises. The card above is postmarked 1928.

CHICKEN RANCHES DOMINATED PETALUMA. In 1896, with his neighbors, Harrison Mecham formed the Poultry Keepers Association (PKA). Organized to fight hen rustling, the PKA expanded to investigate cold storage and organize cooperatively. In 1916, a larger group banded together in a marketing cooperative called the Poultry Producers of Central California (PPCC). The PPCC sent trucks out each morning to pick up eggs from participating farms, which were then brought to the plant and candled, graded, and packed for same-day shipping. From 1915 to 1930, eggs shipped from West Coast co-ops sold under the brand NuLaid to East Coast markets such as New York after the San Francisco market was saturated. By the spring of 1937, the PPCC was selling 60 percent of eggs produced in Petaluma. Two prominent, successful hatcheries are shown in these images. Sales & Bourke, above, formed in 1935 when the Must Hatch and Sales hatcheries merged. The interior of the Bihn Hatchery is pictured below.

Decline of the Poultry Industry. In 1913, the poultry industry slumped but rebounded during World War I. It tanked again during the Great Depression, when many smaller operations went out of business. Larger ranches persisted and then flourished during World War II, when demand was high. In 1919, the Petaluma Incubator Company went bankrupt, owing $35,000 to the Sonoma County Bank and lesser amounts to over 70 creditors. In the 1950s, rapid changes to the poultry industry left Petaluma behind. Cheaper factory farms with indoor chickens in wire cages sprang up in the Central Valley and Southern California. Urbanization precipitated by the post–World War II population influx made it very profitable for Petaluma farms to be subdivided for housing. In 1958, the Poultry Producers Cooperative, formerly called the PPCC, transferred its egg processing plant to San Leandro and ultimately failed in 1963 due to changes in the industry and alleged mismanagement. In 1958, Petaluma's first hatchery, the Pioneer, closed following Eric Nisson's death. In 1989, H&N International, the last remaining hatchery in Petaluma, ceased operation. This card, postmarked 1920, reads, "Dear Grandpa—Thought you would like to see what a chicken ranch looks like again."

Six

The World's Egg Basket

Promoting Petaluma

Promoting Petaluma. Trying to emerge from a post–World War I slump, local business owners sought a new endeavor to stimulate Petaluma's economy. To that end, the Petaluma Chamber of Commerce hired Herbert W. "Bert" Kerrigan to promote Petaluma. Kerrigan devised a marketing plan to pitch Petaluma as the "World's Egg Basket," capitalizing on the local poultry industry. The campaign was successful, spawning efforts like the creation of a National Egg Day in 1918, the annual election of an egg queen, and the Egg Day parade. The image on this postcard was the cover of the Petaluma Chamber of Commerce's 1921 booklet.

HOME OF THE LITTLE WHITE HEN. Publicist Bert Kerrigan's advice to the Petaluma Chamber of Commerce was to "stick with what you already know and promote it to the hilt." And promote it did. The postcard above of a float in a parade was taken in front of the Palace Hotel in San Francisco in 1918 in an attempt to promote egg consumption and encourage more ranchers to settle in Petaluma, which Kerrigan tagged "home of the little white hen." Two men pictured in the foreground are Hiram Hopkins (left) of McNear's feed and Bert Kerrigan (right). Kerrigan found parades to be effective publicity. Note that the float below boasts that Petaluma has 5.45 million hens producing 528 million eggs annually for $13.2 million, which is a higher volume—but lower value—than the float originally showcased in San Francisco (above). (Above, courtesy Craig Blackstone; below, courtesy Petaluma Museum.)

GIANT HENS. The float above included not only the egg basket, but also a giant White Leghorn hen named Chanticline. Note that at the time of the parade, Petaluma was boasting higher production—now six million hens laying 600 million eggs. The image below is of the same giant hen, Chanticline, placed in front of the Petaluma railroad depot (around 1930) to advertise that Petaluma now had 10 million hens to lay eggs. Note the old Petaluma Hotel in the background at right.

VAUNTED EGGS. Eggs alone were featured in some of Kerrigan's promotions, including this giant egg basket that was installed to the south of the Petaluma railroad depot. This basket, reportedly 15 feet long by 10 feet wide and 5 feet high, visually made the point that Petaluma had an extra-large egg production capacity.

THE HEN THAT LAID 1,000 EGGS. This popular postcard promoted eggs and the poultry industry in Petaluma. In theory, high-producing hens, like White Leghorns, can lay more than 1,000 eggs in their lifetime. Generally, in commercial facilities, hens are culled earlier once their annual production starts to taper. The hen pictured here, whether or not she truly laid 1,000 eggs, clearly provided good publicity for Petaluma.

SUCCESSFUL PROMOTION. The Petaluma Chamber of Commerce aggressively promoted the town, as evidenced in this postcard showing the depot with the giant chicken statue and a floating egg basket in the sky. Petaluma was promoted as a tourist destination in close proximity to San Francisco, a prime spot for relocation, and as the "World's Egg Basket." (Courtesy Craig Blackstone.)

PROMOTION IN THE CITY. In 1923, the Petaluma contingent at the American Legion Convention in San Francisco included "Petaluma Chickens" (women dressed as hens, carrying egg baskets). This and similar promotions paid off; within the first six months of Kerrigan's Petaluma publicity campaign, reportedly at least 60 new families moved to Petaluma to begin poultry farming. The town and related industries boomed.

Petaluma Loves a Parade. There were numerous parades in Petaluma in the early years. The image above, postmarked April 30, 1910, says on the back, "This card is a photo during the 4th of July festival in Petaluma. This is Main St., running down 3rd." The image below shows the "Red Cross Parade" in 1918 on Kentucky Street. Petaluma's first Egg Day parade was held in 1917, with the parade route publicized in the *Argus*. (Below, courtesy Sonoma County Library.)

EGG DAY. Part of Kerrigan's promotion of Petaluma was to support the creation of an official annual national Egg Day. To that end, he declared an Egg Day first in 1917, which was promoted in San Francisco and celebrated on August 13, 1918. That year, and for the years following on the third weekend in August, Petaluma celebrated Egg Day for several days. The postcard on this page depicts a "Parker Baby Aeroplane" ride at an Egg Day celebration in the early to mid-1920s. Parker billed itself as the "World's Largest Builders of Amusement and Ride Devices," a perfect addition to the festivities in Petaluma. Newspapers from various cities, including Riverside, Stockton, and San Luis Obispo, promoted the Egg Day festivities held in Petaluma.

Egg Day Parade. Petaluma celebrated its first annual Egg Day and Exhibition from July 1 to July 4, 1916, which was followed by the patriotic Fourth of July parade. However, Kerrigan's successful pitch to exploit this publicity opportunity amped up the festivities. From 1917 until about 1925, Petaluma's Egg Day celebration included parades, carnivals, circuses, rodeos, free barbecues, and extensive contests, including best egg recipes, tug-of-war, and best downtown window displays. Stunts and gimmicks became more spectacular annually. Egg royalty, in later years named "Queen Hen-rietta" and "King Chant-I-Clear," presided over events such as a National Egg Luncheon, the Grand Parade of the Ancient Order of Eggs, and grand balls. (Courtesy Sonoma County Library.)

Petaluma Boosters. This image shows an Egg Day parade entry that promotes both Petaluma as the "World's Egg Basket" by the Petaluma Ad Club and the Pacific Telephone and Telegraph Company Bell System long-distance telephone. A contingent of employees is dressed as telephone receivers and telephone poles.

Egg Day Floats. Local businesses got into the act to promote themselves as they celebrated Egg Day. The float above is a recreation of the steamer *Gold*, advertising the Petaluma & Santa Rosa Railroad Company. The float below, a "Modern Brooder House," was presented by the Camm & Hedges Company, one of the multiple manufacturers of incubators and brooders in Petaluma at the time. Note the live chicks fenced in on the front of the float. (Both, courtesy Sonoma County Library.)

Egg Day Legacy. The float depicted in this 1923 image shows an ostrich chick hatching from a giant egg, being pulled by men dressed as roosters. It was sponsored by the Petaluma Incubator Company and demonstrates how elaborate the festivities had become. Kerrigan resigned as manager of the chamber of commerce in 1924 as it became clear all the promotional activities (including grand plans for renovating Kenilworth Park) had put the chamber into debt. Members had to pay their dues three to four years in advance to cover the financial obligations. While Petaluma continued to own its identity as the "World's Egg Basket," zany promotional antics toned down. That is, until 1981, when Linda Buffo, downtown merchant, and Alice Forsyth, who worked for the Downtown Merchants Association, resurrected the parade and christened it the Butter and Egg Day Parade to be inclusive of the region's dairy industry. (Courtesy Petaluma Museum.)

Seven

Numerous Recreation Facilities

Hotels, Entertainment, and Clubs

Unique Theatre. A 1921 Petaluma Chamber of Commerce brochure boasted, "Numerous recreation facilities are close at hand." Located on the east side of Fourth Street between B and C Streets, the Unique Theatre was one of Petaluma's leading entertainment venues. It opened as Turner Hall in 1875 and was renamed the Unique Theatre in 1904. At one point, the town's first skating rink was located here. The American Legion Post moved into the building in 1921 and stayed until 1965, after which the structure was demolished. (Courtesy Petaluma Museum.)

HILL OPERA HOUSE. The theater at Washington and Keller Streets was commissioned by the Hill family and designed by Charles Havens, who also designed the Silk Mill in Petaluma. The popular venue for plays and musicals held its first performance on December 6, 1904, and was the "Pride of Petaluma" until the early 1920s, when it was destroyed by fire.

CALIFORNIA THEATER. In 1925, Hill Opera House became the California Theater, acquired by T & D Jr. Enterprises, a company that operated more than 60 theaters in the 1940s. This 1940s postcard showcases the large marquee. The theater seated more than 1,200 people and was rebuilt after a fire in 1957. It was renamed the Showcase Theater and, later, the Phoenix Theater in 1979.

Golf and Country Club. The 1922 Arts and Crafts–style wooden bungalow was designed by Brainerd Jones; the property includes a nine-hole course with wide panoramic views. Although modest compared to other private clubs, it had all the important amenities of a social club, such as a bar, deck, and social hall. The building went through substantial renovations in the 1950s. This postcard, postmarked 1932, reads, "This is our golf club house, with Mr. McNear looking out over the course which he gave to us. (the land, I mean)."

Petaluma Woman's Club. The club was established in 1895 and first called the Ladies Choral Society. In 1900, it was admitted to the California Federation of Women's Clubs. This Craftsman-style stucco building with Prairie-style windows was commissioned by the club and completed in 1914. Designed by Brainerd Jones and located at 518 B Street, the interior space includes a large wood-paneled room with a stage and a kitchen. This postcard is dated 1917.

Odd Fellows at Night. The Petaluma chapter of the Independent Order of Odd Fellows (IOOF) was founded in 1854. The Second Empire–style building with a mansard roof on Main Street is one of the oldest commercial structures downtown, built in 1871. It was built on the site of Petaluma's first hotel, the Petaluma House, constructed in 1852. In 1926, the Odd Fellows incorporated the adjacent building on the north, including a single facade. (Courtesy Sonoma County Library.)

American Hotel Lobby. Hotels, many starting as boardinghouses, have been part of Petaluma since the very beginning. The first American Hotel building at this location was erected by George Williams as a four-bedroom boardinghouse in 1852, until it burned in 1868. The hotel was rebuilt with brick but burned again in 1873. This postcard mailed in 1912 is of the lobby of Petaluma's third American Hotel, constructed in 1873 on Main Street north of Western Avenue. (Courtesy Lew Baer.)

Third American Hotel. The new American Hotel included a saloon, barbershop, restaurant, and movie house during the 1930s. The three-story hotel was also known for its bus service to the train station. The hotel was remodeled several times before being condemned and demolished in 1966. The empty lot turned into a passageway to Kentucky and Keller Streets, known as the Golden Concourse walkway. In 1987, the space was dedicated as Helen Putnam Plaza. (Courtesy Petaluma Museum.)

Cosmopolitan Hotel. On the left of this postcard mailed in 1907 is the Cosmopolitan Hotel, a 40-room working man's hostelry. The town attracted many single men seeking business or employment opportunities. These hotels provided short-term and long-term accommodations for those not able or desiring to build their own house. The hotel site is now a vacant lot and famous for the "police axle stunt" in the 1973 movie *American Graffiti.*

CONTINENTAL HOTEL. The Continental Hotel was previously known as the City Hotel, which is speculated to be a hotel structure built in Chile and first moved to the town of Vallejo before moving to Petaluma in 1853. The building on Western Avenue between Keller and Kentucky Streets was remodeled and renamed the Continental in 1905. The 60-room hotel was condemned when it burned in 1968. (Above, courtesy Lew Baer; below, courtesy Petaluma Museum.)

HOTEL PETALUMA. The success of the poultry industry led to the need for better accommodations for visitors and businesses. This five-story fireproof steel and concrete Mediterranean-style hotel with a mission tile roof opened on April 22, 1924, at the corner of Western and Kentucky Streets. Designed by Frederick Whitton, a San Francisco architect, it included a spacious lobby, large fireplace, and a mezzanine floor. The hotel featured 96 guest rooms with 12 employee rooms on the top floor. The hotel was community funded; the chamber of commerce launched a campaign to sell shares, resulting in 855 local investors. The luxurious hotel also became a gathering place for social events and civic meetings. The modern kitchen served the elegant dining hall that seated up to 200 people. The hotel had the first passenger elevator in Petaluma. The building sold to the Petaluma Elks Lodge in 1959, and the Elks occupied it for the next three decades.

Hotel Petaluma Front Entrance. The main entrance on Kentucky Street leads into an elegant courtyard with a water fountain. In 1938, the area was enclosed and converted into the Lanai Lounge, a popular coffee shop and cocktail lounge with Polynesian decor and tropical drinks. Tiki lounges became popular as a way to experience the atmosphere of the islands. The Lanai Lounge was considered Petaluma's version of the Tango Room or Trader Vic's in San Francisco. (Courtesy Petaluma Museum.)

First Frame House Site. The hotel is also the location of one of Petaluma's first wood-frame houses. The Douglas family brought their house from Maine by ship and assembled it there in 1851. The home was also used as a boardinghouse. Two of the streets nearby the Hotel Petaluma are named after the Douglas family's daughters, Mary and Martha. This postcard of the hotel was mailed in 1939.

The Redwood Room. This double-wide card is postmarked 1947. Aldo Lazzarini painted this mural in 1945 in what became the popular Redwood Room at the Hotel Petaluma. The 150-seat Redwood Room replaced the Lanai Lounge as the popular nightspot in the hotel. In 1959, the new tenants of the building, the Elks Lodge, converted the Redwood Room into retail shops. The mural was preserved by relocation to the Petaluma Historical Library and Museum.

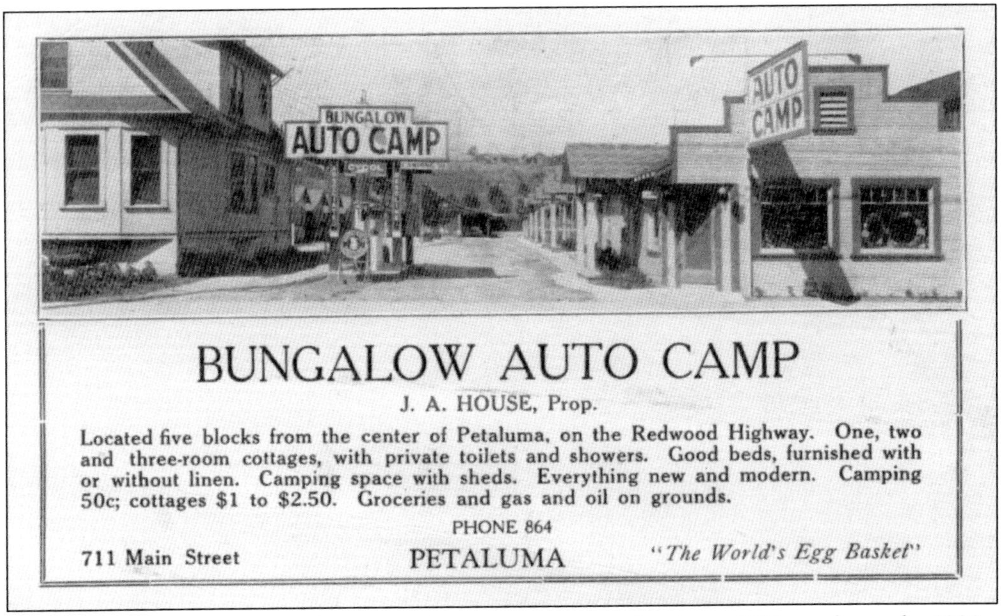

Bungalow Auto Camp. Auto camping was very popular from 1913 to the early 1920s. Americans became automobile owners and found a new sense of freedom with the ability to drive away and travel. The auto camps were precursors of motels and recreational vehicles. This Petaluma camp was located on the west side of Main Street between West and Cherry Streets, just a few blocks from downtown. (Courtesy Petaluma Museum.)

Casa Grande Motel. The proliferation of cars and recreational outings led to the need for roadside lodging. This motor court on Petaluma Boulevard between E and F Street opened in 1948. The back of the postcard, sent in 1967, says, "In downtown Petaluma, the New Casa Grande Motel. 35 miles north of San Francisco. Comfortable Single and Double Units, Free TV, Owner Operated." Later, the motel was demolished, and it turned into a vacant lot.

Eight

Civic and School Advantages

Public Institutions

Free Public Library. The Petaluma Chamber of Commerce boasted about the town's "Civic and School Advantages" in a 1947 brochure. The Carnegie Library, built in 1906, reflects the influence of the "City Beautiful" movement created by Chicago's World Columbian Exposition of 1893, featuring grand-scale classical buildings. This effect is enhanced by the Neoclassical–style building's elevated placement at the corner of Fourth and B Streets. Local architect Brainerd Jones designed a two-story portico with Corinthian columns that provides an entrance into a wood-decorated interior with a vaulted ceiling covered with a stained-glass dome.

PETALUMA'S CITY HALL. The public building was designed by prominent architects Samuel and Joseph Newsom from San Francisco. The Victorian brick building was completed in 1887 and stood on Kentucky Street. The two-story building with a basement housed the city courts, administrative offices, and public library as well as police and fire services. In 1955, the decorative and elegant building was demolished and replaced with a parking lot.

EARLY FIRE COMPANIES. As flame was used for lighting and heating, and many of the early structures were of wood, there was a constant risk of fire, and many buildings perished during those early years. In 1857, some 40 citizens organized the Petaluma Volunteer Engine Company No. 1. By 1880, Petaluma had six volunteer fire companies covering various parts of the town as well as competing to be the first on the scene of a fire. In 1910, James Mott became the first paid firefighter in Petaluma. A few years later, the volunteer groups dissolved and the city took over firefighting. The above postcard is of the city's famous fire horse, Black Bart, pulling the fire carriage parked alongside the steps of city hall, which housed the Petaluma Fire Department in the early 1900s. By 1919, motorized fire trucks had replaced the horse-drawn carriages. (Below, courtesy Sonoma County Library.)

OLD POST OFFICE. The Neoclassical-style building on Main Street with Gothic Revival–style columns, designed by Brainerd Jones, was built in 1926 and served as Petaluma's post office until 1932. The yellow bricks were manufactured at George P. McNear's brickyard in San Rafael, and the material for these unusually colored bricks came from Alameda. The Sierra National Bank used the building until the 1970s, after the post office moved to Fourth Street. (Courtesy Sonoma County Library.)

NEW POST OFFICE. The well-preserved Spanish Colonial Revival structure on Fourth Street was designed by James Wetmore and Louis Simon and became Petaluma's new post office. It was funded by the Keyes-Elliot Act in 1926 and completed in 1933. The front of the building consists of five arches that form the central portion of the post office. The six gargoyle downspouts are placed in between the arches and provide a unique Spanish Gothic element.

Mutual Relief Building. The Mutual Relief Building was erected in 1885 in the Italian Renaissance architectural style at the corner of Kentucky Street and Western Avenue. The three-story building is considered a treasured landmark for its beautiful style but, more importantly, for its use of cast iron for the facade. The Mutual Relief Association was a community life insurance organization that formed in 1870. Private mutual aid societies proliferated nationally in the late 19th century to provide social welfare as public aid was reduced. Private efforts became less necessary after Pres. Franklin D. Roosevelt signed the Social Security Act in 1935. The back of the Petaluma building has the historical Coca-Cola wall advertisement painted on the brick exterior wall.

B Street Grammar School. The Red Brick School was dedicated on February 11, 1860, and was considered one of the finest school buildings in the state and the first brick schoolhouse constructed in Sonoma County. The two-story building with a capacity of around 250 children was designed by Brainerd Jones and located on Fifth and B Streets. It was demolished in 1911 to make room for a new school, the Lincoln Primary School, also designed by Jones. (Courtesy Petaluma Museum.)

Early School History. Schools have been an integral part of Petaluma's history. The earliest school gatherings were in the early 1850s, and Petaluma was identified in a county school report as having its own school district in 1854. The school census of 1863 counted 521 children. The first private high school, shown in the middle of this multiview postcard, was built by Prof. Edward S. Lippitt in 1867 on D Street, near Sixth Street. In 1873, the building was purchased by the school district and became Petaluma's first public high school.

Pepper Free Kindergarten. A private school opened at the southwest corner of Liberty and Washington Streets in 1894, with an enrollment of 28 pupils. The Pepper Free Kindergarten was founded by William H. Pepper, who owned a successful nursery and orchard business. Interestingly, a young Luther Burbank was briefly one of his employees. Traveling in Europe, Pepper was inspired by the German kindergarten system, which was free to the public. He donated the land and contributed significant financial support with the intent of providing free kindergarten to all Petaluma children, a novel idea at the time. The Greek Revival–style school building was torn down in 1960, and the school continued at a different location.

PETALUMA'S SECOND HIGH SCHOOL. This image shows the town's second Petaluma High School building, constructed in 1889 on Keller Street between Oak and Prospect Streets. This was the beginning of significant growth in Petaluma, and the school structure was able to serve the education needs of the town for several decades. Students organized themselves into societies. The Everett Society chose white as a color, and the Irving Society chose purple, which explains the origin of the Petaluma High School colors. The school building was torn down in the 1920s.

WASHINGTON GRAMMAR SCHOOL. The school was built in 1905 on Post Street between Bassett and English Streets, also known as Bassett Street Plaza, after the passing of a $35,000 bond. The 10-room school was designed by Henry Smith and Louis Stone, San Francisco architects that specialized in designing schoolhouses. The building was purchased by the city in 1950 and subsequently demolished to make room for the Petaluma Civic Plaza.

McKinley School. A 1910 bond allowed for the construction of two new schools, McKinley School and Lincoln Primary School. The McKinley School was designed by Brainerd Jones in the Craftsman style and replaced the Washington Street School. The school was torn down in the 1950s, and a new school was built on Ellis Street. On the back, the postcard reads, "This is the school in east Petaluma."

Lincoln Primary School. The Greek Revival–style building designed by Brainerd Jones replaced the B Street Grammar School. The new school boasted an updated heating and ventilation system, modern sanitary facilities, and an auditorium. In 1955, the building was converted to house the administrative offices of the Petaluma City Schools. After four decades, the offices were relocated, and the building was converted for commercial use.

THIRD HIGH SCHOOL. The third high school in Petaluma was designed by Brainerd Jones and located on Fair Street. The two-story brick building was completed in 1915 and equipped with the most modern features and conveniences. Due to earthquake damage and the need for a larger facility to accommodate increased enrollment, the building and several surrounding residences were torn down in 1958. The grounds that the high school occupies was once the location of the Sonoma and Marin Agricultural Park, where the annual fair was held. Petaluma was the only public high school in town until Casa Grande was established in 1972 on the east side of town.

Junior High School. This building was located on Fair Street between English and Bassett Streets and was designed by Brainerd Jones in 1922. The school occupied an entire block and included a gymnasium. The school was able to alleviate the congestion at the senior high school on Keller Street. The junior high was torn down in 1960 to create playing fields for the new high school.

Junior High and High School. This image shows Webster Street in the foreground and Bassett Street on the left, extending to St. Vincent de Paul Roman Catholic Church. On the left of Bassett Street at Fair Street is the backside of the junior high school, which was demolished in 1960. On the far right is the backside of the high school, which was removed in 1958.

Petaluma High School Athletics. Petaluma High School has a long history of athletics, with football being played sporadically as early as the 1890s. Girls' basketball was formed in 1907. Track and field was one of the first sports at Petaluma High School in 1915, along with basketball and baseball. The old Petaluma High School track was half a mile long until it was rebuilt in the late 1940s as Durst Field and renamed Ellison Field in 2012.

Petaluma High School Pennant. The first leather postcards were produced in 1903 and typically made of deer hide, with the image burned into the leather. They became popular when people started sewing them together to make pillows or wall hangings. The US Postal Service banned leather postcards in 1907, when too many became caught in the sorting machines. They continued to be made as souvenir cards until 1910. This one proudly shows a Petaluma High School pennant. (Courtesy Craig Blackstone.)

Two Rock School. Small schoolhouses in the countryside outside Petaluma were quite common. The Two Rock School was established in 1885 and located 12 miles west of Petaluma, in the rural area. In 1919, it was merged with two other schools to become a single school district, Rock Hill Union School District. A new school was built at this five-acre location on Spring Hill Road in 1952. (Courtesy Petaluma Museum.)

Waugh School. The one-room school, known as Bethel School, at Corona and Adobe Roads, was built in 1863 by Lorenzo Waugh. The Methodist minister and his wife, Clarissa, arrived in California in 1852 from West Virginia and were granted 320 acres from General Vallejo. It was reported to be the first country schoolhouse in Sonoma County and became a public school in 1897. It was replaced with the Waugh School building in 1925. (Courtesy Petaluma Museum.)

Union School House. This wood-framed building with a bell tower was rebuilt in the 1890s across the street from its original location. The original San Antonio School was built in 1858 next to a social hall on Red Hill Road (D Street extension) but was destroyed by fire. In 2010, it became one of the few remaining one-room schoolhouses in the North Bay.

Nine

A Strong Moral and Religious Sentiment

Churches

Houses of Worship. A chamber of commerce brochure from 1906, boasting about Petaluma churches, stated that "a strong moral and religious sentiment pervades the city." The first church congregations founded in Petaluma were Methodist in 1849, followed by Baptist in 1853, and then others, including Roman Catholic in 1857. This multiview postcard captured the 10 churches in Petaluma in 1915. They are labeled as Episcopal, Presbyterian, Congregational, Baptist, Christian, M.E. Church South, M.E. Church North, Catholic, Advent, and Lutheran.

METHODIST EPISCOPAL CHURCH. Methodists were the first settlers to organize as a congregation and build a church in Petaluma. This postcard illustrates their second church building on the northwest corner of Western Avenue and Keller Street. The Gothic-style brick building was completed in 1874 and included a gallery, orchestra, and classrooms. The Methodists sold the building in 1940, after which it was demolished. (Courtesy Sonoma County Library.)

METHODIST CHURCH. The merging of three Methodist branches in 1939 provided the resources to purchase a site at Fifth and D Streets, which was once the location of John A. McNear's home. The United Methodist Church was designed by Vincent Raney, a prolific San Francisco architect of theaters. The church held its first service in the new building on December 7, 1941, the same day the Japanese attacked Pearl Harbor.

FIRST CONGREGATIONAL CHURCH. This High Victorian Gothic Revival–style church located on Fifth Street was built in 1901 and replaced the Congregational church from 1857. The First Congregational Society of Petaluma was organized in 1855 and met at various homes for the first couple of years. Some of the striking features of this second church from 1901 are the main tower with its pyramidal roof, the large rose window donated by John A. McNear, and the arched windows and door openings. The postcard below shows the sanctuary before the extensive interior remodeling in 1945. The wooden structure, with detailed boards and friezes, was sold in the 1960s.

THE FIRST BAPTIST CHURCH. The second-oldest church in Petaluma was built in 1857 on Kentucky Street, near Prospect Street. The First Baptist Church became famous for the purchase of its historical bell, which was used in San Francisco to call the Vigilante Committee in 1858. The church's large steeple was often used as an orientation point for surveys. It was the oldest Baptist church in California when demolished in 1910 to make room for a new church.

BAPTIST CHURCH. In 1911, new leadership led to the decision to remove the old building and replace it with a brick and stone structure. A Neoclassical-style church designed by Brainerd Jones and built by Vogensen Construction Company replaced the wood-framed church in 1911 at its location on Kentucky Street, across from Hill or Upper Plaza Park, now Penry Park. The "Church on the Hill" was torn down in 1965, as it had outgrown the space, and a new Baptist church was erected on Webster Street. (Courtesy Lew Baer.)

CHRISTIAN CHURCH. The Christian Church of Petaluma was established in 1883 and incorporated a few years later. This building on Western Avenue and Post Street was completed in 1911 and served as the congregation's second church until 1971. The building was sold to the city when the congregation relocated to their new church on Schuman Lane. The property served as a community center and was renamed the Polly Hannah Klaas Performing Arts Center in 1994. (Courtesy Petaluma Museum.)

Old St. Vincent de Paul Roman Catholic Church. There were many Roman Catholic churches in California, starting with the Spanish missions. St. Vincent's was the first in the town of Petaluma. This is the second church, a Gothic Revival–style structure built in 1876 at the corner of Western Avenue and Bassett Street. The first church was a wooden structure built at the southeast corner of Keokuk and Prospect Streets as soon as the Catholic parish was formed in 1857. (Courtesy Craig Blackstone.)

Interior of Old St. Vincent's. This 1910 postcard provides a unique glimpse into the sanctuary. In 1925, the Gothic-style church was sold to the Elim Lutheran Church. That congregation dismantled and reconstructed the building on land they purchased at the corner of Baker and Stanley Streets. One-third of the materials were used to rebuild the church. The sanctuary lamp and large church bell were saved and used in the building of the new and much larger Catholic church, which remained at the same location on the corner of Western Avenue and Bassett Street.

ST. VINCENT'S CONVENT. This three-story brick masonry structure, with a small dome on the roof, was designed by Thomas Welsh and constructed in 1888 at Union and Howard Streets. The Italian Renaissance Revival–style building served as both a school and a convent until 1916, when a separate convent was constructed. The second floor was removed in 1937, and substantial renovations were made for an elementary school. The St. Vincent's Convent building was condemned in 1989 but brought back up to code afterward.

St. Vincent de Paul Roman Catholic Church. The Spanish Colonial– and Romanesque Revival–style building was designed by San Francisco architect Leo J. Devlin. In 1926, Fr. James Kiely had raised enough funds to build the new church, and his experience from the 1906 earthquake led him to request a double steel reinforced frame. The first service was Christmas midnight Mass in 1927. The impressive building that dominates Petaluma's townscape has a clay tile roof, two bell towers topped with mosaic tile work, three arched entrance doors, and a large rose stained-glass window. The interior includes three marble altars, the sanctuary lamp from the previous church, a number of stained-glass windows and solid oak pews. The church can accommodate up to 1,000 people.

St. Vincent's Renovation. In 1916, a Craftsman-style rectory and hall were built behind the church structure. Until the 1990s, the church's color was a single pale beige color. Multicolor painting was introduced during major restorations in the 1990s. In 2001, a pedestrian plaza with a fountain was created in front of the church, allowing for integration with Liberty Park.

St. John's Episcopal Church. St. John's Episcopal congregation in Petaluma was established in 1856 and started with a small wooden church. It was replaced in 1890 with the distinctive Shingle building designed by Ernest Coxhead, an English-trained architect influenced by the British Arts and Crafts movement. This influential architect combined several architectural styles for the church, including Baroque, Romanesque, and Gothic.

Christian Science Church. The first Christian Science services in Petaluma were held in 1906 and continued at various town locations. In 1917, the lot at B and Sixth Streets was purchased, and the congregation used a Victorian house on the land for the next five years before building their own church. In 1922, this Spanish Colonial Revival–style church was completed with traditional stucco walls and a Spanish tile roof.

Ten

Playgrounds for the People

Homes and Public Parks

Views of Petaluma. The chamber of commerce produced a brochure in 1914 boasting about Petaluma, including its many parks—"playgrounds for the people." The elegant homes and large mansions built at the turn of the 20th century are testimony to Petaluma's early success and prosperity. This postcard showcases the Camm House and the Fairbanks Mansion built on D Street. John Camm was the president of Camm & Hedges, a successful lumber and planing mill. The Camm House was completed in 1906 and designed by Brainerd Jones in the Stick and Tudor architectural style. (Courtesy Craig Blackstone.)

THE HEALEY RESIDENCE. The Dennis and Margaret Healey home, built in 1902 at the corner of Washington and Keokuk Streets, was designed by local architect Brainerd Jones. Dennis Healey was a local businessman who owned the Petaluma Furniture Company. It was demolished in 1969 after the Sorenson Funeral Home occupied it for several decades. The community responded by organizing to recognize and preserve heritage homes.

THE FAIRBANKS MANSION. This postcard, mailed in 1909, is of the three-story Queen Anne–style home built for Hiram Fairbanks and his wife, Lucinda, in 1890. The house on D Street is reflective of the wealth of a successful Petaluma businessman. The 8,500-square-foot Victorian-style house includes beautiful interior woodwork, nine bedrooms, seven baths, and a wraparound porch. The house used to encompass the entire block and included a carriage house and formal gardens. (Courtesy Craig Blackstone.)

HOMES OF BODEGA AVENUE. The houses built in the country tended to be more modest. The photograph for this postcard of a two-story house from 1900 on Bodega Avenue was captured by well-known photographer Ella Jorgensen from Tomales. The covered porch, gable roof, and double-hung windows draw from the Queen Anne–style architecture. A Mrs. Turner writes on the back of the postcard, "Sending you a picture of my home, my quarters are upstairs and I rent out the lower floor."

WORKING-CLASS HOMES. This postcard is another example of a modest house in Petaluma from the early 1900s. The need for affordable housing was important to accommodate the new families arriving in Petaluma who were looking for work and business opportunities. The planting of palm trees at the time was quite common for ornamental purposes, as they provided neither shade nor edible fruit.

UPPER OR HILL PLAZA. A plaza in the tradition of Mexican and Spanish towns resonated with Petaluma's early settlers. The Upper Plaza, first referred to as Main Street Plaza, became a public space in the initial town surveys of 1852. After decades of neglect, the Ladies Improvement Club, formed in 1896, led efforts to improve the Upper Plaza (renamed Hill Park) and the Lower Plaza (renamed Walnut Park). This postcard above reads, "This is a beautifully laid out park. The band is played there every day during the summer." The Ladies Improvement Club transformed the plaza into a park by removing old trees, installing gravel paths, placing benches, and planting palm trees. The postcard below provides a view of downtown from the northwest corner of the park looking along Kentucky Street. Now named Penry Park, it has still has the original layout of the paths.

Upper Plaza Parking. This postcard was mailed in 1911 and provides a view of the southeast corner of the Upper Plaza Park. It shows the retaining wall of granite stones along the banked hillside and the land that was removed along Mary Street to accommodate for hitching horses and wagons. More land was removed in the 1960s to accommodate additional street parking.

Penry Park. In 1929, this French 75-mm field gun was placed above the marble World War I monument. The field gun in this postcard was replaced with two 37-mm anti-tank guns in 1949. In 2001, the park's name was changed to Penry Park in memory of Army sergeant Richard Penry of Petaluma, who received the Medal of Honor during the Vietnam War. (Courtesy Petaluma Museum.)

Walnut Park. The block was originally purchased in 1873 by the city with support from local businessperson John A. McNear. There were many community plans and financial contributions to maintain D Street Plaza, but few were fully implemented until 1896. At that time, the Ladies Improvement Club made what became Walnut Park its second park project. The need for irrigation led to the construction of a well, windmill, and tank house.

Hebe Fountain. In 1891, the Women's Christian Temperance Union worked on the installation of the large decorative fountain near Main and Washington Streets. It was to be moved to Hill Park Plaza in 1927 but was moved to Walnut Park instead. In the late 1800s, many temperance fountains, including Hebe Fountains, were placed by the women's group in parks across the country to encourage water, as opposed to alcohol, consumption. The fountain was removed by the 1960s. (Courtesy Petaluma Museum.)

Walnut Park and the Public Bandstand. The above postcard was mailed in 1906, several decades before the bandstand was built. This view of the park is from D Street, looking toward Fourth and E Streets. The large house in the background on the right is the home of Henry and Addie Atwater on Fourth Street. Addie was president of the Ladies Improvement Club and responsible for the creation of Walnut Park. The postcard below is of the public bandstand. The gazebo, located in the middle of the park and dedicated in 1927, was designed and built by the Petaluma Lions Club. The structure had a concrete base with columns and a railing and included a roof with sunken lights. The musical concerts from the bandstand in the park were popular for decades. The community park was also used for political rallies, movie locations, and public markets.

Oak Hill Park. The large site was the town cemetery until the 1870s, after which it was made into a park through a community effort in 1908, when the Oak Hill Improvement Club, another women's civic group, began turning it into Petaluma's third park. The enhancements included paths and benches, but unlike the other Petaluma parks, the natural vegetation remained. The tree sign in this postcard, mailed in 1911, says, "No fire arms or shooting birds allowed on these grounds under penalty."

Old Kenilworth Park. In 1920, the largest auto camp in California at the time opened in Petaluma at Kenilworth Park, a site used previously as fairgrounds as well as for a horse track and stables. Kenilworth is the name of the Thoroughbred racehorse of the farm and the landowner, Harry Stover. The park on East Washington Street provided shade trees, white tables, camp stoves, and a children's playground. A decade earlier, the citizens of Petaluma voted for the city to purchase the 80-acre parcel to become a municipal park and continue its use for agricultural events. The fairgrounds and the park became an important location for countywide celebrations.

PARK AT LOWER MAIN. This postcard from the early 1900s shows an open space at the south end of Main Street with hitched horses and wagons surrounding a group of trees. This unusual plot located in the center of town was modified into a small park around 1921 and became known as Center Park. This early postcard provides a view looking south down Main Street with a rare glance of the Unique Theatre, located at Fourth Street between B and C Streets, in the background on the right.

CENTER PARK IN THE 1920S. This view of a developed Center Park shows the marquee of the Mystic Theater on the left and, to its right, the landmark McNear Building. The McNear Building was constructed in 1886 by John A. McNear, Petaluma's most significant developer at that time. The high Victorian Italianate commercial building, with cast-iron false fronts, faces both Main Street and Fourth Street. The Mystic Theater was built in 1911 and was a popular venue for vaudeville shows.

CENTER PARK IN THE 1940S. Also referred to as Plaza Park, Center Park is now one of Petaluma's smallest parks. In 1977, a replica of the Mission Trail Bell was placed at the north end of the park to commemorate Petaluma's location on El Camino Real, the route traveled between the missions by the Spanish missionaries. A second commemorative mission bell is housed inside the Petaluma Historical Library and Museum. Center Park anchors one end of the iconic historic downtown, which illustrates part of what gives Petaluma so much reason to be proud.

Bibliography

Biddie, George, ed. *Western Poultry History.* Sacramento, CA: Pacific Egg and Poultry Association, 1989.

Cassiday, Samuel. *An Illustrated History of Sonoma County.* Chicago, IL: Lewis Publishing Company, 1889.

Hansen, Harvey J., and Jeanne Thurlow Miller. *Wild Oats in Eden: Sonoma County in the 19th Century.* Santa Rosa, CA: Hooper Publishers, 1962.

Heig, Adair. *History of Petaluma: A California River Town.* Petaluma, CA: Scottwall Associates, 1982.

Heritage Homes of Petaluma. Petaluma, CA: Heritage Homes of Petaluma, 1978–2002.

Hess, Scott, and John Sheehy. *On a River Winding Home: Stories and Visions of the Petaluma River Watershed.* Penngrove, CA: Ensatina Press, 2018.

History of Sonoma County. San Francisco, CA: Alley, Bowen & Company, 1879.

Illustrated Atlas of Sonoma County California. Santa Rosa, CA: Reynolds & Proctor, 1897.

Lowry, Thea. *Empty Shells: The Story of Petaluma, America's Chicken City.* Novato, CA: Manifold Press, 2000.

Petaluma Argus-Courier (1928–2020).

Peterson, Dan. *Petaluma's Architectural Heritage.* Santa Rosa, CA: Architectural Preservation Associates, 1978.

Rinehart, Katherine J. *Petaluma: A History in Architecture.* Charleston, SC: Arcadia Publishing, 2005.

Schmale, John and Kristina. *Petaluma and Santa Rosa Railway.* Charleston, SC: Arcadia Publishing, 2009.

Thompson, Robert A. *Historical and Descriptive Sketch of Sonoma County, California.* Philadelphia, PA: L.H. Everts & Company, 1877.

Wilson, Simone. *Petaluma, California.* Charleston, SC: Arcadia Publishing, 2001.

Index

About the Petaluma Historical Library and Museum

PETALUMA
MUSEUM
ASSOCIATION

The former Carnegie Library now houses upstairs in its permanent collection Petaluma poultry, dairy, and Miwok Indian history exhibits, while the main floor hosts a series of topical exhibits throughout the year. The cornerstone was laid in 1904, and the library opened in 1906. The building, designed by local architect Brainerd Jones and constructed from locally quarried stone, features the largest free-standing leaded glass dome in Northern California. The building is in the Neoclassical style, featuring original fan-glass windows, round leaded-glass windows, and original interior wood paneling and columns. It also houses a research library that features an invaluable treasure trove of historical documents and photographs. Please visit our website for current exhibits and activities.

The Petaluma Historical Library and Museum
20 Fourth Street
Petaluma, CA 94952
(707) 778-4398
petalumamuseum.com

The Petaluma Historical Library and Museum is dedicated to "Preserving the Unique History of Petaluma and Providing Educational and Cultural Services to the Community."